Hotel Galvez · Queen of the Gulf

A CENTURY OF HOSPITALITY ON THE TEXAS GULF COAST

GARY CARTWRIGHT

NEW COLOR PHOTOGRAPHY BY CAROL M. HIGHSMITH

HOTEL GALVEZ AND SPA
GALVESTON, TEXAS

For Tam, my beautiful and perfect wife. —Gary Cartwright

Published by

Mitchell Historic Properties

2228 Mechanic Street, Suite 204, Galveston, Texas 77550
409-763-5806
www.mitchellhistoricproperties.com

for the

Hotel Galvez & Spa
A Wyndham Grand Hotel

2024 Seawall Boulevard, Galveston, Texas 77550
409-765-7721
www.WyndhamHotelGalvez.com

Copyright © 2010 by Mitchell Historic Properties

All rights reserved. No part of this book may be reproduced or transmitted in any form or by any means, electronic or mechanical, including photocopying, recording, or by an information storage and retrieval system, without permission in writing from the publisher.

ISBN 978-0-578-05858-0

Printed in Singapore

Book project managers for Mitchell Historic Properties:
Renee Adame, Director of Marketing and Special Projects
Christine Hopkins, Public Relations Manager

Research by Larry Wygant

Produced by
Archetype Press, Inc.
Diane Maddex, Project Manager
Robert L. Wiser, Designer

Contents

FOREWORD · PETER H. BRINK · 14

Introduction
DANCING WITH HISTORY · 18

Queen of the Gulf
THE QUEEN'S CASTLE · 25
DOWN MEMORY LANE · 30
COMING FULL CIRCLE · 42

"A Kind of Magic"
THE FREE STATE OF GALVESTON · 51
THE GREAT STORM · 58
PICKING UP THE PIECES · 62
A LANDMARK RISES · 65
THE GRAND SYMBOL · 67

America's Treasure Island
THE GANGS OF GALVESTON · 81
NEW HANDS ON DECK · 87
WINDS OF WAR · 88

Misfortune and Rebirth
STORMY YEARS · 93
FROM SKID ROW TO HISTORIC DISTRICT · 96
"GOOD ENOUGH FOR EVERYBODY AND NOT TOO GOOD FOR ANYBODY" · 104
SOUP'S ON! · 108

Ghosts and Other Guests
BIG SHOTS · 114
THE GHOST BRIDE OF ROOM 501 · 116
THANKS FOR THE MEMORIES · 119

MILESTONES · 130
ACKNOWLEDGMENTS · ILLUSTRATION CREDITS · 131

SUN PARLOR, HOTEL GALVEZ, GALVESTON, TEXAS.

Interior View of Ballroom, Hotel Galvez, Galveston, Tex.

Foreword

Galveston is imprinted on the national consciousness because of the devastating hurricane of September 8, 1900, which brought with it the largest number of deaths from any natural disaster in the United States. Miraculously more than a thousand structures survived this deadly storm.

Also miraculous was Galveston's response to the disaster: building a massive seawall, raising the level of much of the city with fill barged in from nearby bayous, and constructing a magnificent resort hotel. The Hotel Galvez, completed in 1911, was undertaken by Galveston leaders as a community effort. The six-story hotel overlooking the Gulf of Mexico was built to be Queen of the Gulf, and indeed it was. It became the premier choice for wedding celebrations, honeymoons, and other special occasions, taking its place as part of the lives and memories of thousands of guests.

However, Galveston—once Texas's busiest port—was eclipsed by Houston's massive deepening of its ship channel in 1914 and the subsequent rise of the Port of Houston. The vision of Galveston as a leading commercial center thus died, and the city went through decades of little or no growth. This situation in turn allowed one of the finest collections of Victorian architecture in the country to remain intact. Publication of *The Galveston That Was* in 1966 became a wake-up call for preserving this architectural treasure. In the early 1970s Galveston looked to historic cities such as Savannah, Georgia; Charleston, South Carolina; and San Antonio as its inspiration. Through the leadership of scores of Galvestonians and other Texans, along with the participation of thousands, Galveston has realized the value of its historic neighborhoods and landmarks. It has become a national leader in saving and reusing thousands of historic structures, from Victorian mansions, Carpenter Gothic houses, and modest cottages to the cast-iron commercial structures of The Strand, including the rebirth of The Grand 1894 Opera House and the living maritime heritage of the 1877 barque *Elissa*. George P. Mitchell and the Mitchell family have been seminal leaders in this effort, serving by far as the largest owners and restorers of buildings on The Strand.

The Hotel Galvez is a beacon in this community renaissance. The hotel had fallen into bankruptcy in 1988, and a few years later George Mitchell, at the urging of his wife, Cynthia, purchased the hotel and began the process of restoration. George and Cynthia's driving vision was always to return the Hotel Galvez to the Queen of the Gulf that it once was. They have succeeded magnificently. Gary Cartwright's splendid narrative is a living testament to Galveston as one of America's special places and to George and Cynthia as people who have made a truly magnificent difference in the historic city they have long loved.

Peter H. Brink
Former Executive Director, Galveston Historical Foundation, and
Former Vice President for Programs, National Trust for Historic Preservation

Introduction

Dancing with History

Strolling through the magnificent lobby of the Hotel Galvez and Spa, visitors sense that they are dancing with history—and that history is leading. Here one can feel the same island rhythms that Cabeza de Vaca, La Salle, and Jean Laffite probably felt in their bones centuries ago, taste the same salt breeze, hear the same pounding surf. Through the great arched windows of the hotel's twin loggias, looking south beyond the stand of stately date palms and trim beds of oleanders that announce the hotel's main entrance on Seawall Boulevard, lines of waves break along the beach, just as they have for thousands of years.

The carpeted loggias—with their high ceilings, graceful arches, and chandeliers of electric candles—run east to west, along the front of the U-shaped hotel. This brilliantly lighted central corridor, with its chandeliers reaching for the sun like brass blossoms, must have been familiar to Frank Sinatra, Peggy Lee, and other celebrities who stayed here when they played the Balinese Room across the boulevard. Generals Douglas MacArthur and Dwight D. Eisenhower may have sat in heavy wicker chairs and overstuffed couches similar to the furniture in place today. When he was a senator, Lyndon B. Johnson stayed at the Galvez. So did Richard Nixon. So did Douglas "Wrong Way" Corrigan, a Galveston native and well-known aviator who became infamous in 1938 for flying his small plane to Ireland rather than Long Beach, California, as he had intended. Howard Hughes secluded himself in one of the Galvez's penthouse suites. In the spring of 1937, President Franklin D. Roosevelt made the hotel his official Summer White House for ten days while he fished and stayed aboard his yacht, the U.S.S. *Potomac*. But the Galvez was the place where F.D.R. got his mail—so it is fun to think that the president might have mailed a postcard in the antique gold-plated mailbox next to the elevators.

For nearly one hundred years, since June 10, 1911, the Galvez has stood its ground on this high piece of real estate above the Gulf of Mexico, flanked by Twenty-first Street, Avenue P, and Seawall Boulevard. The hotel was built in the wake of the nation's greatest natural disaster, the Great Storm of 1900, which killed an estimated six to eight thousand Islanders and devastated the city of Galveston. Its construction was the

Right: Despite the surging hurricane of 1915, the Hotel Galvez weathered the storm—thanks to the new seawall. Opposite: The Felix Stella Orchestra, a popular Galveston band, provided music for guests during the hotel's first decade.

apex of a daring and unprecedented building program that also included erecting the seawall and elevating the grade level of the entire city. From the moment it was born, the Galvez was recognized as one of the great resort hotels in the South, not to mention one of the most audacious challenges to the forces of nature. It became the center of social life in Galveston, indeed in all of Texas. Dignitaries and political rainmakers gathered in its lobby and bar to plot the fate of the world. Its ballrooms hosted thousands of proms, coming-out parties, and weddings—to this day the hotel hosts an average of 135 weddings a year. The bandleader Phil Harris and the actress Alice Faye married in the seventh-floor penthouse of the gangster-entrepreneur Sam Maceo, who with his older brother, Rosario "Rose" Maceo, ruled over the Island's economic and moral climate (the rackets) for a quarter century beginning in the 1930s.

But the Hotel Galvez also played memorable roles in the lives of thousands of ordinary people, some of whom have sent along their recollections for publication in this book (see page 119). A promotional brochure published at the time of the hotel's grand opening boasted that it was "Good enough for everybody and not too good for anybody." In those salad days following the grand opening, honeymooners, vacationers, and even business types from all over the country gathered on the south lawn, on wooden swings or benches, to watch the tropical moon or to listen to the roar of the waves—perhaps wondering what would happen when the next big hurricane hit the Island.

They found out in 1915, just four years after the Galvez opened. The storm hit with such fury that it hurled four-ton blocks of granite riprap across the boulevard and lifted a three-masted schooner out of the water and tossed it over the seawall. The storm flooded downtown, blew out windows, and demolished nearly all the buildings beyond Fifty-third Street. Although more than three hundred persons died on the mainland and on Bolivar, only seven perished on Galveston Island. The seawall had done its job.

Legend has it that as the storm ravaged the Texas coast, guests at the Galvez drank champagne and danced the night away in the hotel's ballrooms.

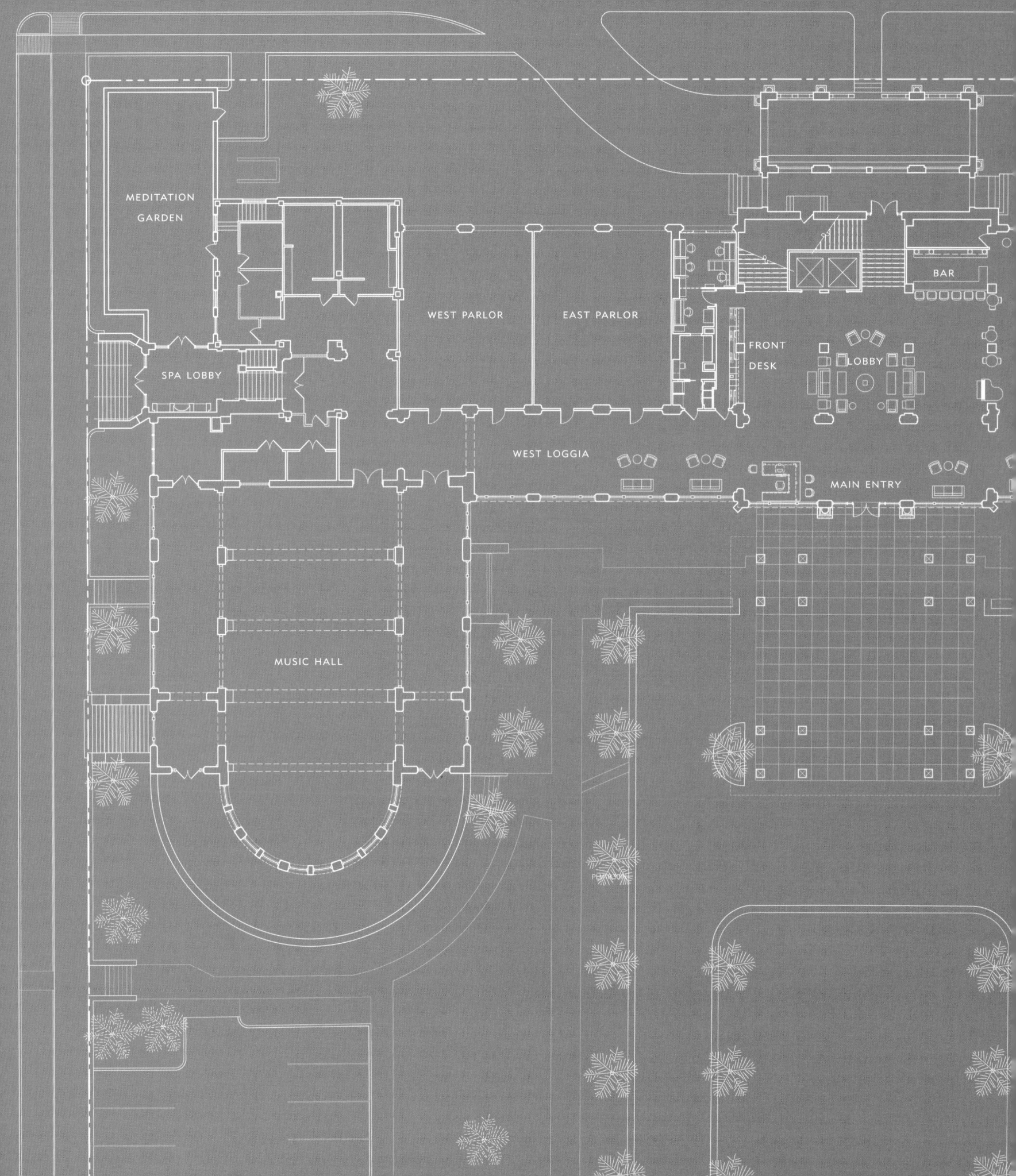

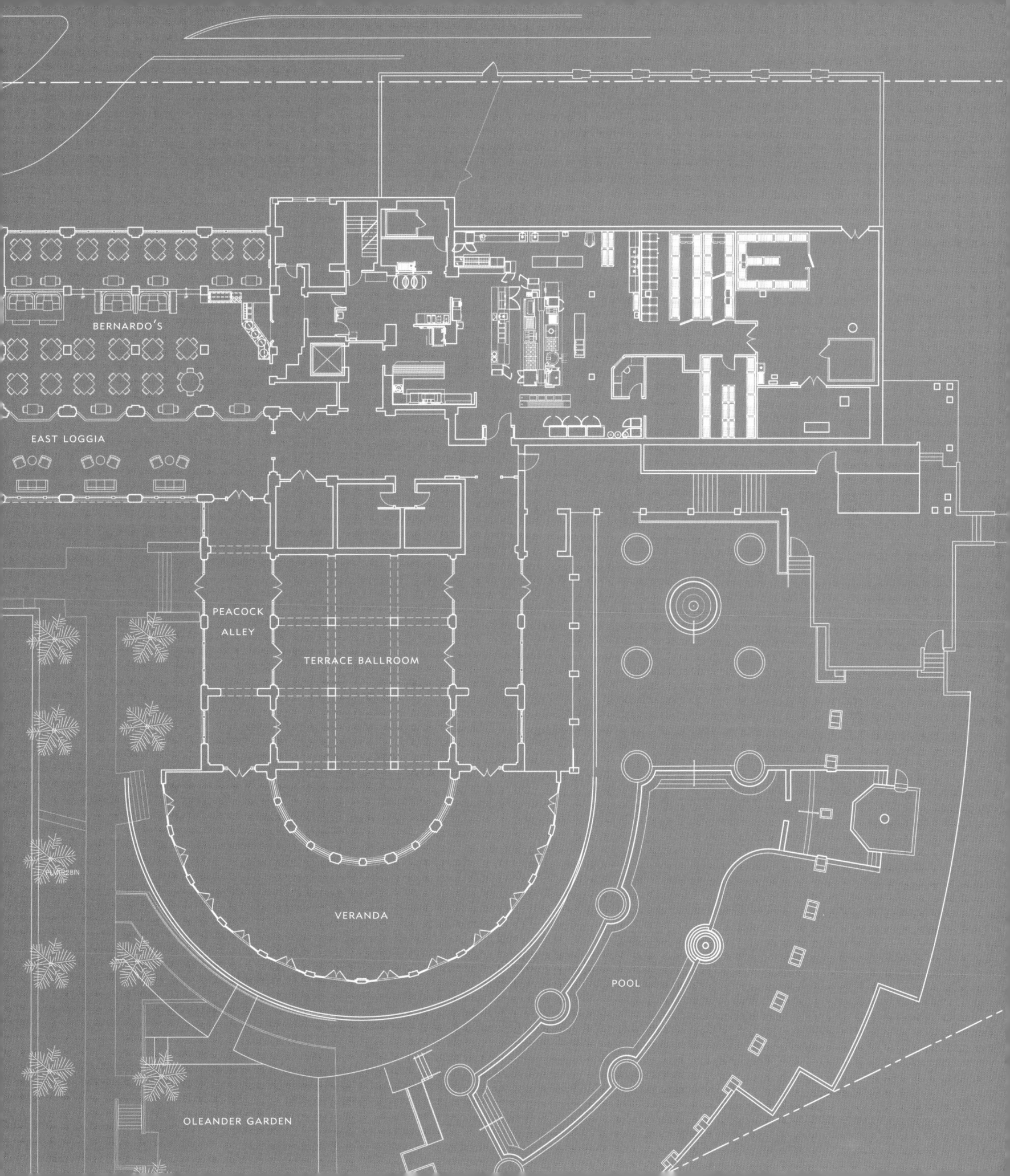

Queen of the Gulf

The Queen's Castle

To appreciate the Galvez in all its grandeur—to understand why it is called Queen of the Gulf—one should view the hotel from the sidewalk along Seawall Boulevard. The Galvez dominates the eastern end of the Island in the way a queen's castle dominates her fiefdom. A six-story stuccoed brick building with creamy lime plaster, the hotel features a central section that rises to eight stories under a hipped roof. On either side are two wings whose glassed-in semicircular bays project outward toward the Gulf, one on the west holding the Music Hall, the other on the east holding the Veranda and the Terrace Ballroom. On the wings' gabled roofs are inset mission-style parapets, which are key elements of the building's blended Spanish Colonial Revival and Mission styles. All the overhanging roofs are red tile and low pitched to provide some needed shade. Four hexagonal towers with metal-ribbed vaults define each corner of the central section, whose top-most windows are framed with pilasters and crowned with round arches. A four-story square tower pops up from the roofline above the main section's southeast corner. The hotel is one of Galveston's few buildings showing Spanish architectural influence; the style subtly evokes the state's colonial Mexican heritage and was popular for resorts and railroad stations in the early twentieth century.

Left: As seen from Galveston's beachfront, the Spanish-style landmark is framed by lush lawns and swaying palm trees. Above: A souvenir plate from the hotel's early days emphasizes its proximity to the water.

QUEEN OF THE GULF · 25

Left: In the restored lobby, the beamed ceiling of mahogany is held aloft by sturdy square columns, whose bronze capitals have been meticulously restored to their original appearance. Above: Except for the furnishings, the lobby looked little different when the hotel opened its doors in 1911.

Looking around the lobby, a visitor senses that not much has changed since the hotel opened in 1911. More accurately, almost everything has changed, and changed again, and yet again. But today it looks almost exactly as it did when it opened at 6:00 P.M. on June 10 that year. This is because its current owner, the Houston oilman and preservationist George P. Mitchell—a Galveston native with an outsized love for the island of his boyhood—has returned the Galvez to the grandeur of its original Spanish design. The heavy drapes that once blocked out natural light are gone, bringing the lobby the fresh, bright feeling of being in harmony with the tropics, a captive of the sea's intoxicating perfume. The tone of the supporting columns, topped with bronze capitals, is the original shade of soft gold with white trim—tea and cream, it is called.

Above: In 1911 the Gentlemen's Buffet and Grille Room was a masculine hideaway. Right: Today the bar area, located in the hotel lobby, features the ornate bar purchased from the Old Galveston Club at 2019 Market Street.

The high ceiling of the lobby and the bar area is crisscrossed with heavy mahogany beams. The bar itself is a huge and strikingly ornate piece of handcarved wood, with a giant mirror as its centerpiece. Mitchell purchased the bar from the Old Galveston Club when it closed in October 1992. Rumor has it that the bar, which dates to 1876, once graced the original Tremont House hotel. The club bragged that it was the Island's last speakeasy; in its final years it was dark, smelly, and faintly rancid, like pulverized popcorn ground into the floor of an old movie house, but it spoke with authority when it came to Galveston's heritage. The longtime bartender, Santos Cruz, claimed to have invented the margarita in honor of Peggy Lee when she played the Balinese Room in 1948 (*Margarita* is Spanish for Margaret, Miss Lee's given name). Among the many reasons that the Old Galveston Club was an Island institution was its collection of nude oil paintings of young Galveston women, many from prominent families. Mitchell incorporated the club's bar into the Galvez's decor. Nobody seems to know what happened to the nudes.

Down Memory Lane

Leading away from the lobby, the twin loggias take visitors to the Galvez's two ballrooms: the wide-arched Music Hall in the west wing, which was known as the Grecian Room in the hotel's early days, and the Terrace Ballroom, originally the Terrace Restaurant, in the east wing. The loggias, sometimes called promenades or sun parlors, are lined by great arched windows and furnished with heavy wicker chairs, couches, tables, and potted ferns and plants, just as they were a hundred years ago. Two parlors that were originally designated as the Reading Room and the Writing Room, serving now as meeting rooms, are off the west loggia. When the Galvez opened, these two rooms were part of a larger, more open lobby then called Peacock Alley.

Top: A postcard from about 1911 highlights the unfolding arches that distinguish the Music Hall in the west wing. Above and right: Over the years this space has been the scene of thousands of meetings and social events.

In the spaces above and between the loggia windows are reproductions of the coats of arms of Spanish nobles, in particular Bernardo de Gálvez, a Spanish hero of the American Revolution for whom both this city and the hotel are named. Descended from a long line of Spanish military men, de Gálvez served as a young officer in his country's war against Portugal, was sent to New Spain (Mexico), and was assigned to the faraway province of Louisiana in 1776 and promoted to a colonel of the Louisiana regiment. On January 1, 1777—when he was barely thirty years old—de Gálvez became Louisiana's governor. In the years just before the American Revolution began, de Gálvez corresponded regularly with Patrick Henry and Thomas Jefferson and later commanded Spanish forces in battles against the British along the Mississippi River and the Gulf Coast, winning every battle that he and his Spanish forces fought. Early in 1785, de Gálvez was appointed captain-general of Cuba, Louisiana, and the Floridas, and on his father's death he succeeded to his position as viceroy of New Spain. De Gálvez never saw the island of Galveston himself, but in 1785 he sent an expedition to survey the Gulf Coast. Led by his mapmaker, Jose de Evia, the explorers discovered what turned out to be the biggest bay in Texas. In honor of his commander, Evia named it Bahia de Gálvezton, later altered to Galveston.

Left: Between the arched openings in the twin loggias extending from the main entrance are a series of Spanish coats of arms. Above: Bernardo de Gálvez's motto on his crest is "Yo Solo" ("I alone"). His coat of arms became the hotel's own symbol, featured on the mission parapet of the porte cochere.

Above: Bernardo de Gálvez died in 1786, at the age of forty. His body was laid beside that of his father in the Church of San Fernando in Mexico City, while his heart was placed in an urn and kept at the Cathedral of Mexico, whose completion he had overseen. Right: Bernardo's restaurant celebrates its namesake by offering a menu featuring dishes from the Spanish, Cuban, and Louisiana territories that de Gálvez governed in the colonial era. The restaurant overlooks the east loggia.

On a wall at the bend of the west loggia, between the entrance to the Music Hall ballroom and the steps leading down to the hotel's new spa, hangs a large portrait of de Gálvez, a regal figure in formal military attire. The figure's dark eyes seem to follow visitors as they move along the loggia, giving rise to the legend that the painting is haunted. Haunted or not, the hotel renamed what was originally the Marine Dining Room, calling it Bernardo's in honor of the colonial-era hero.

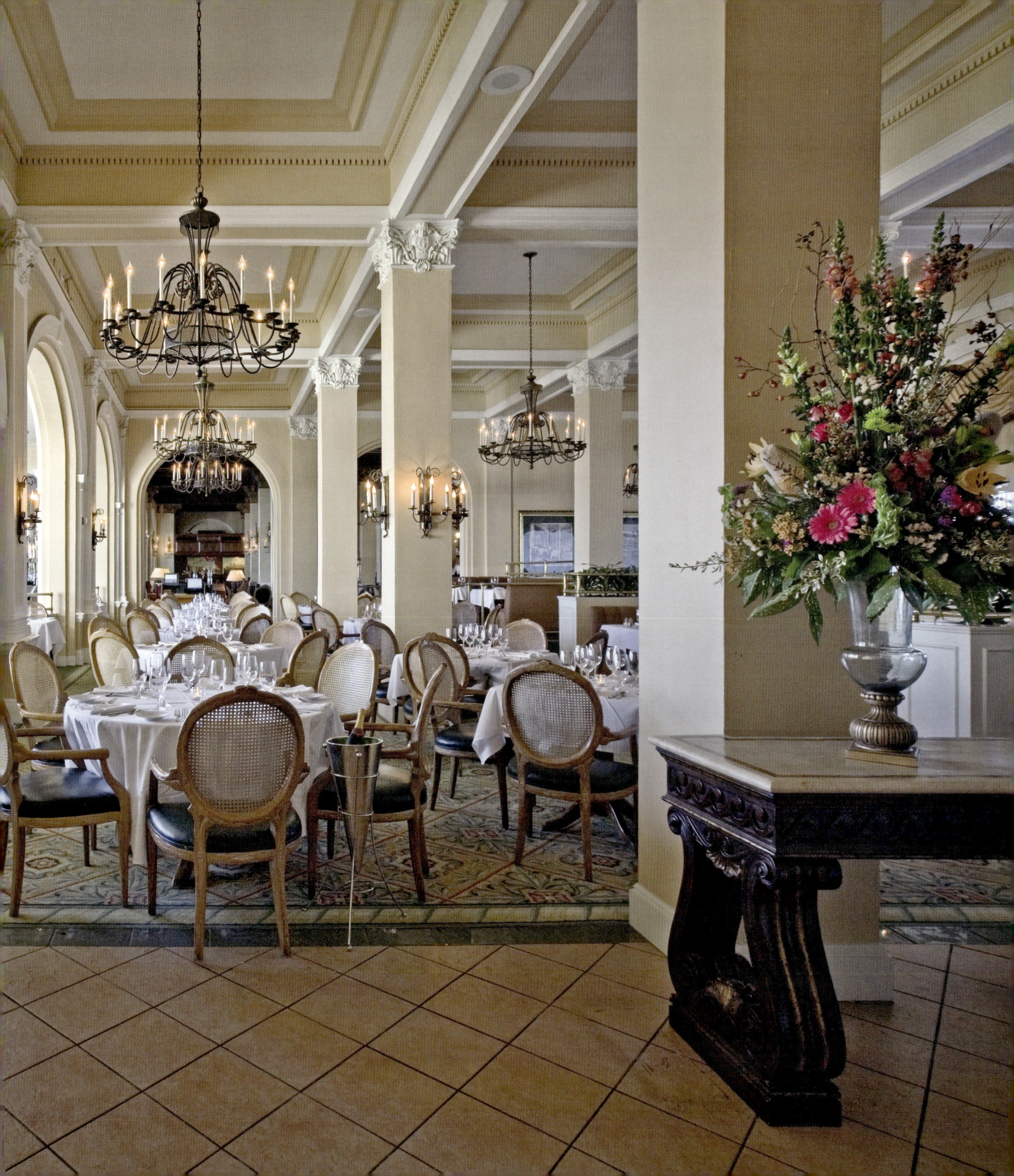

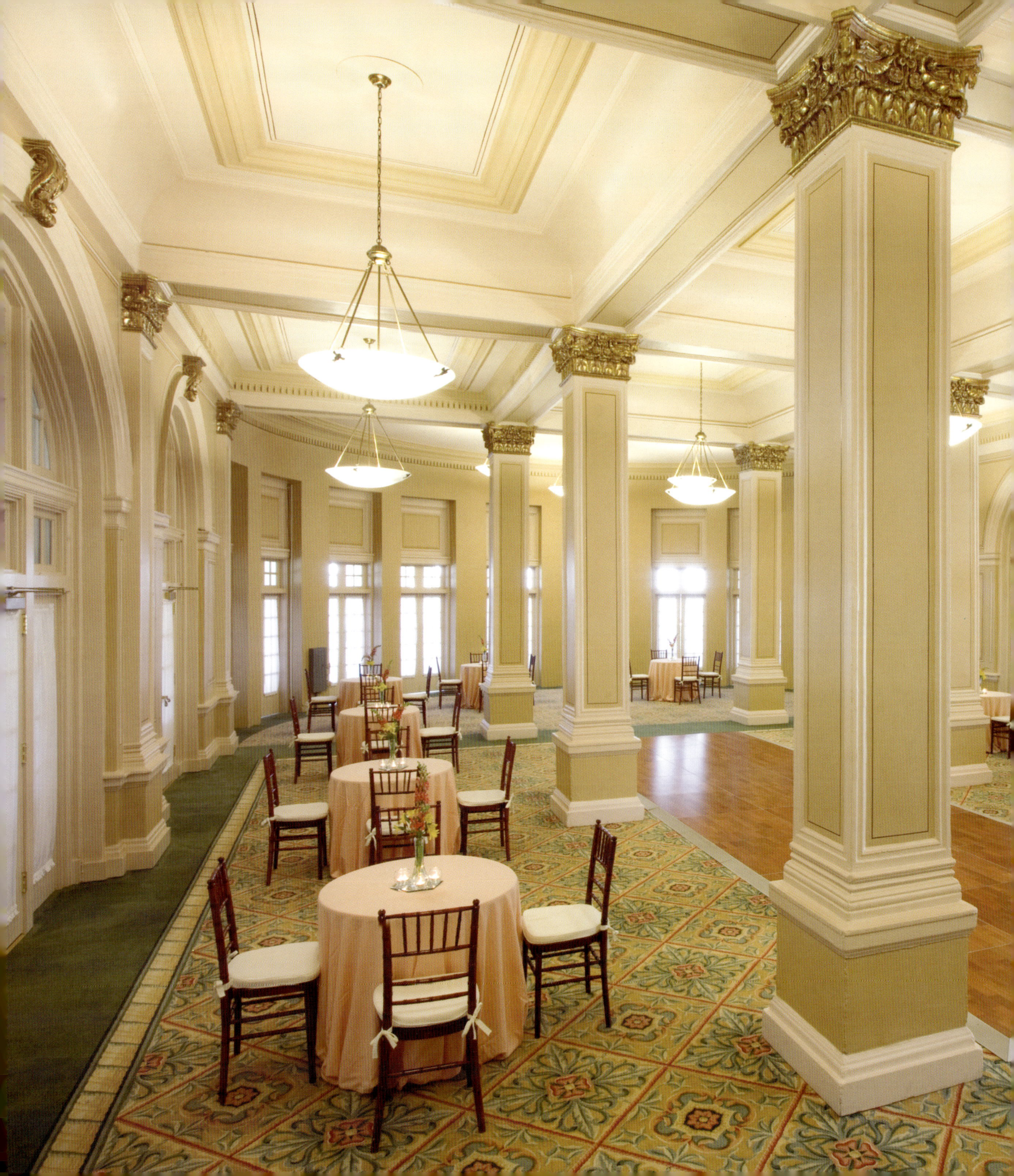

Left: Off the east wing's new Peacock Alley, a corridor connecting with the main lobby, is the popular Terrace Ballroom. Above: In 1911 early hotel guests and visitors dressed in their finery to parade down the original Peacock Alley.

The east loggia winds around to the hotel's opposite wing, where it connects with a companion corridor that has revived the old Peacock Alley designation. The name came from the 1920s generation of visitors, who strutted through the corridor dressed in finery that would shame your average peacock. Men customarily wore suits, vests, and hats, even in summer. Women were photographed in full-length gowns and hats that appeared organic. Today, by contrast, hotel guests are likelier to strut down Peacock Alley in much more casual attire.

Two large rooms open off this corridor: the Terrace Ballroom and another dining area (popular for weddings) known as the Veranda. The Veranda, originally an open-air space, is an airy, bright expanse that curves above the hotel's formal garden, known as the Oleander Garden, and its tropical swimming pool. The area between the east loggia and the exit to the pool was once the Gentlemen's Buffet and Grille, a dark, wood-paneled escape where men could smoke cigars and speak freely of subjects deemed unsuitable for the fairer sex.

Top: The bright and airy Veranda dining area overlooks formal gardens and the tropical swimming pool. Above: Brian and Christine Sorenson add their names to the list of couples who have enjoyed legendary weddings at the hotel. Right: Adjacent to the pool is the Oleander Garden, a popular site for alfresco parties.

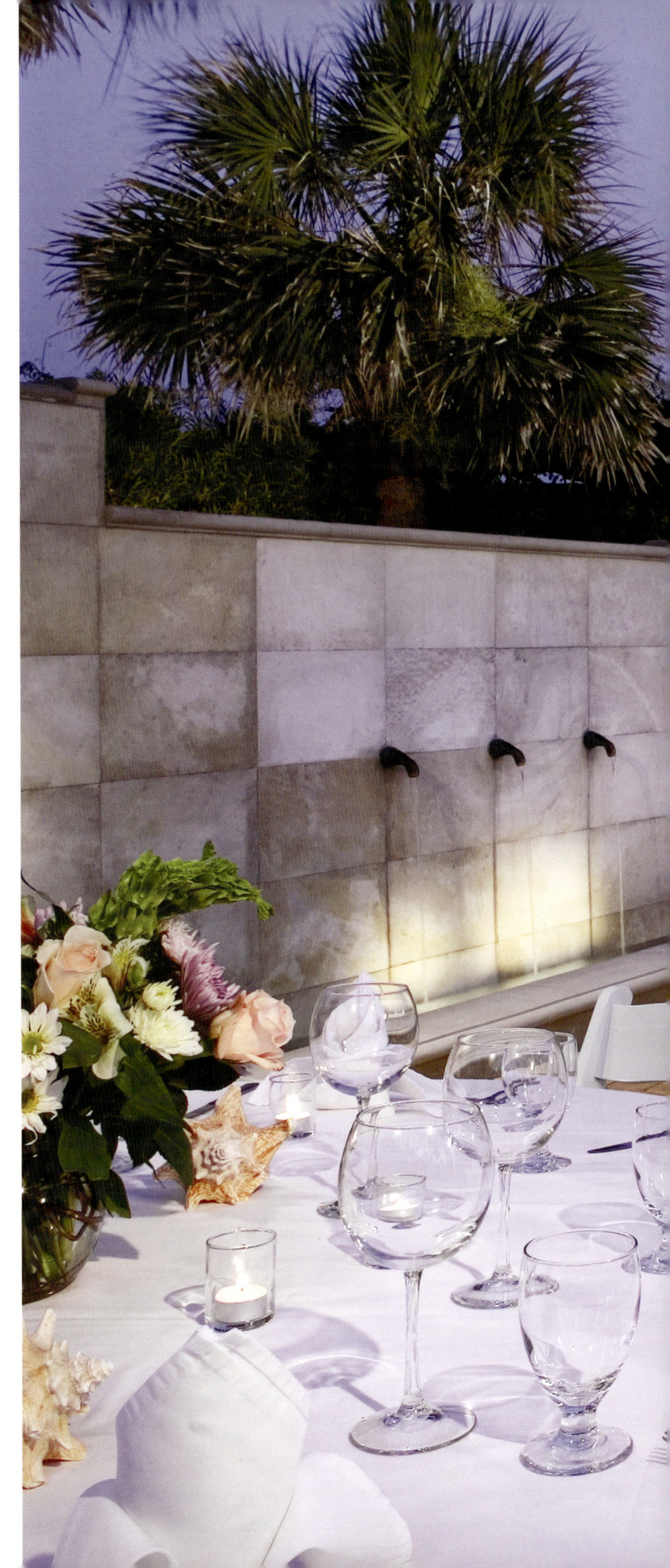

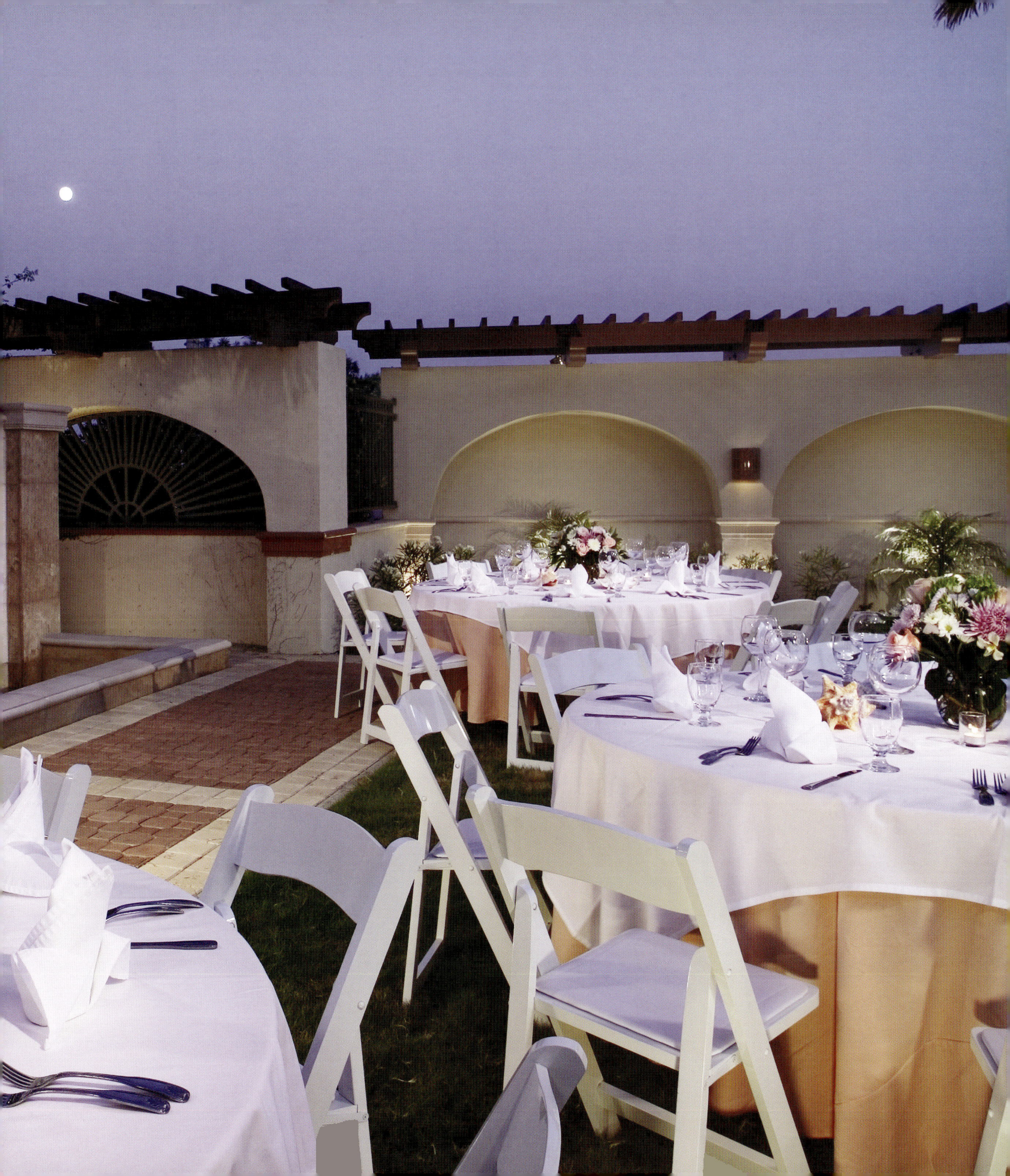

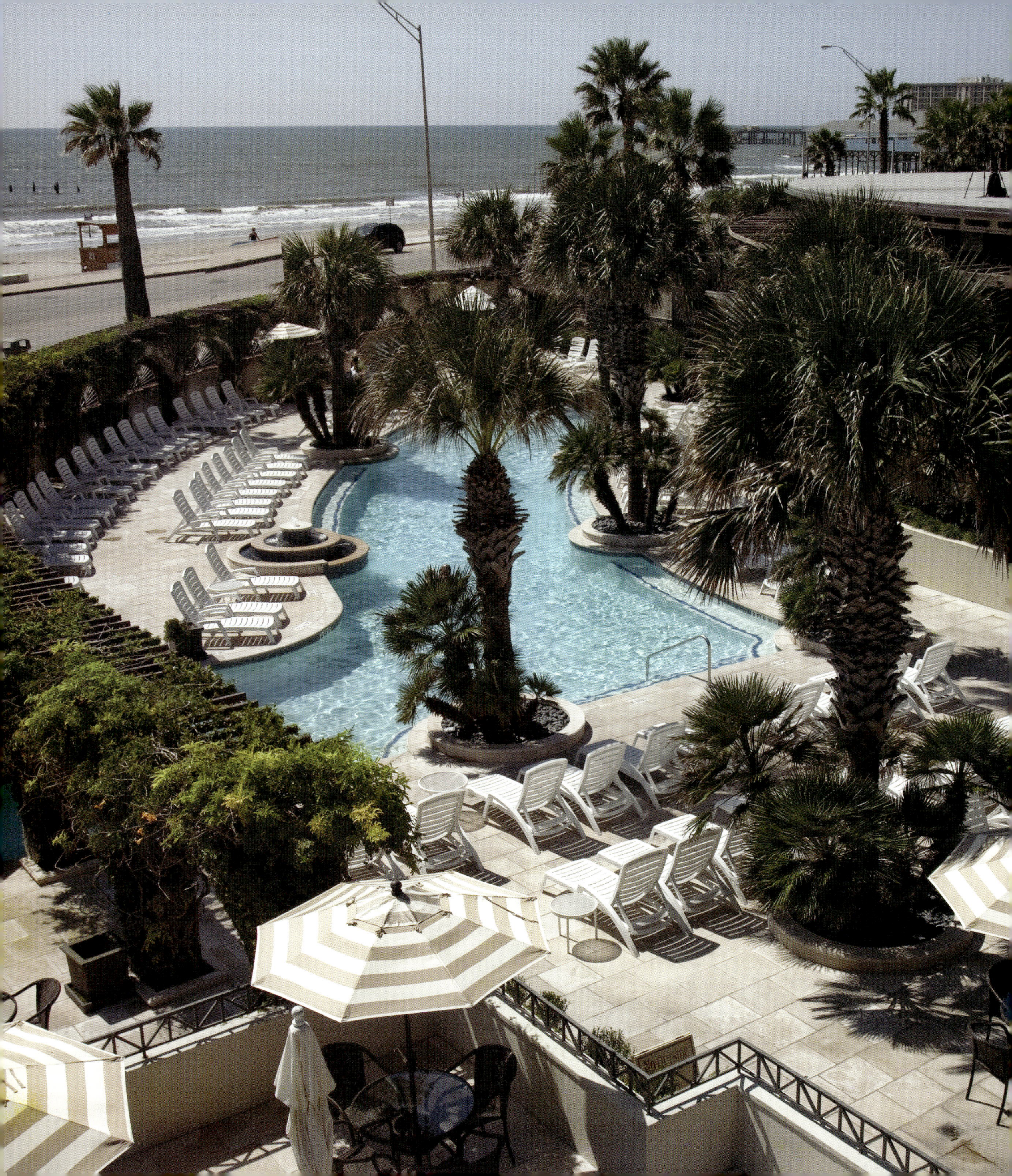

Left: Steps away from Seawall Boulevard and the waves of the Gulf of Mexico is the hotel's tranquil swimming pool, a tropical retreat. Top: Located poolside are several cabanas. Above: A tiered fountain flows into the free-form pool.

COMING FULL CIRCLE

In the early 1990s, George Mitchell's wife, Cynthia, became a driving force in saving and restoring the Galvez. The Mitchell family removed inappropriate additions from 1950–80 and freed up the spacious street-level promenade. And then, in 2005, a second renovation, directed by the Mitchells' daughter Sheridan Mitchell Lorenz of Austin, restored the windows on the lobby level to their original appearance. Heavy drapes that obscured the Gulf view were banished, and plate glass was replaced with divided-light windows. Lorenz also changed the color scheme of the lower level to sunnier, tropical fruit colors to better evoke the hotel's Spanish colonial architectural style. The tea-and-cream color of the columns was traced back to the original color by scraping samples from the capitals in Bernardo's restaurant.

Top: Early visitors with stereopticon viewers could take home their own stereo photograph of the new hotel. Above: Roller chairs allowed early guests to sightsee around the grounds and seawall sidewalks. Right: In the Terrace Ballroom, ornate columns painted in tones of tea and cream revive the hotel's original color scheme.

42 · QUEEN OF THE GULF

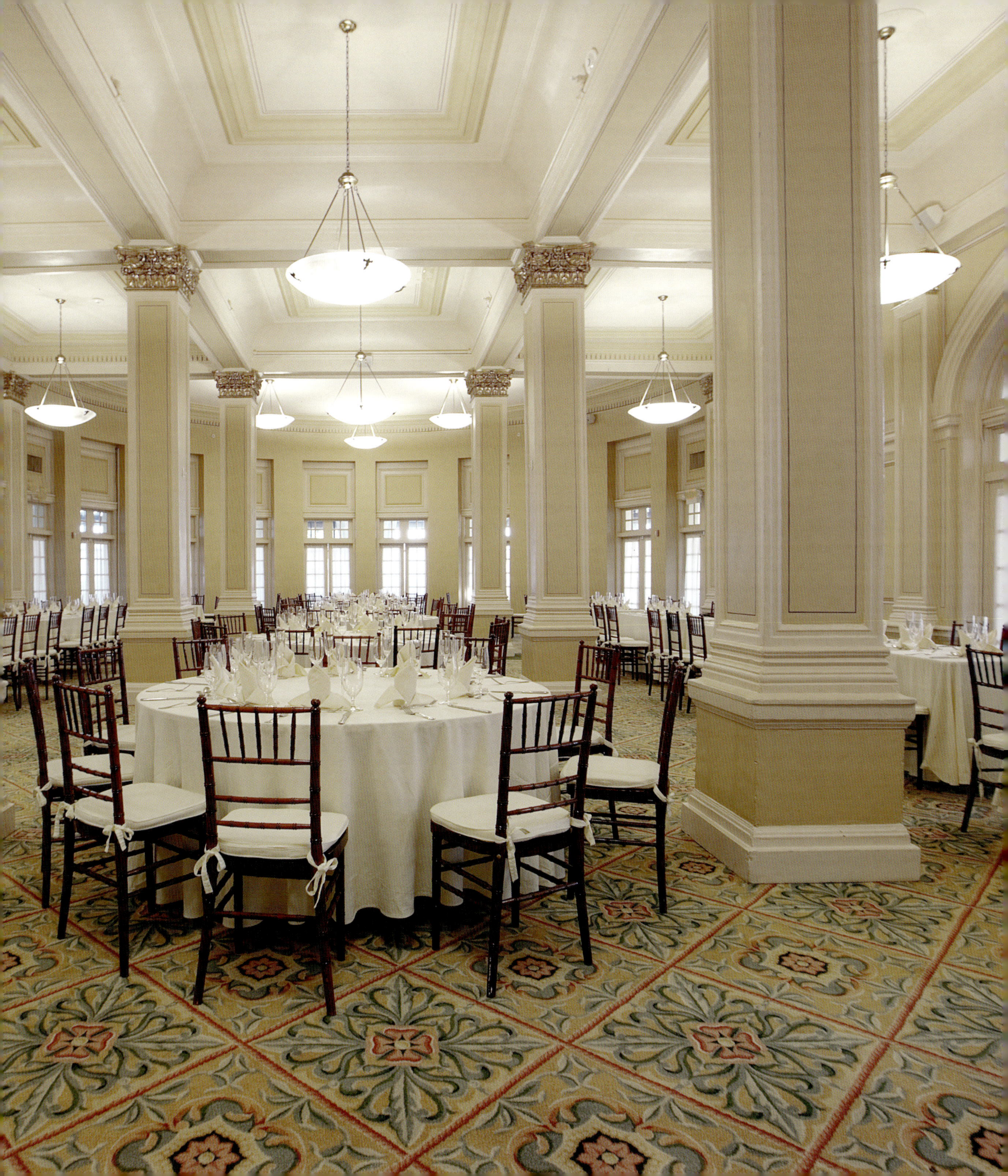

When the Galvez opened in 1911, it offered 275 guest rooms; now the restored hotel has 224 rooms, including six suites. Rooms face either the Gulf of Mexico or the Island (originally the north-facing rooms were used for hotel employees and services). As part of the hotel's centennial, the Gulf-front rooms were updated to feature operable, divided-light windows reminiscent of the original design, and the rooms were updated with a new decor and new furniture. The six suites—all showcase apartments with sitting rooms and baths—are located on the seventh and eighth floors. In addition to the Presidential (701), Hollywood (702), Oleander (703), and Balinese (804) Suites, two suites are named for famous Galvez guests: Roosevelt (802) and Hughes (803). The hotel also features a boardroom honoring General MacArthur.

Top and above: The hotel's 224 newly redecorated guest rooms and suites feature new furnishings, updated bathrooms, and nature-inspired aluminum prints by Kayla Mitchell, granddaughter of George Mitchell. The Gulf-facing rooms offer divided-light windows, reminiscent of the hotel's original design, that can be opened from the top. Right: On the seventh and eight floors, suites such as this have also been updated, while spa-inspired rooms were created on the hotel's sixth floor.

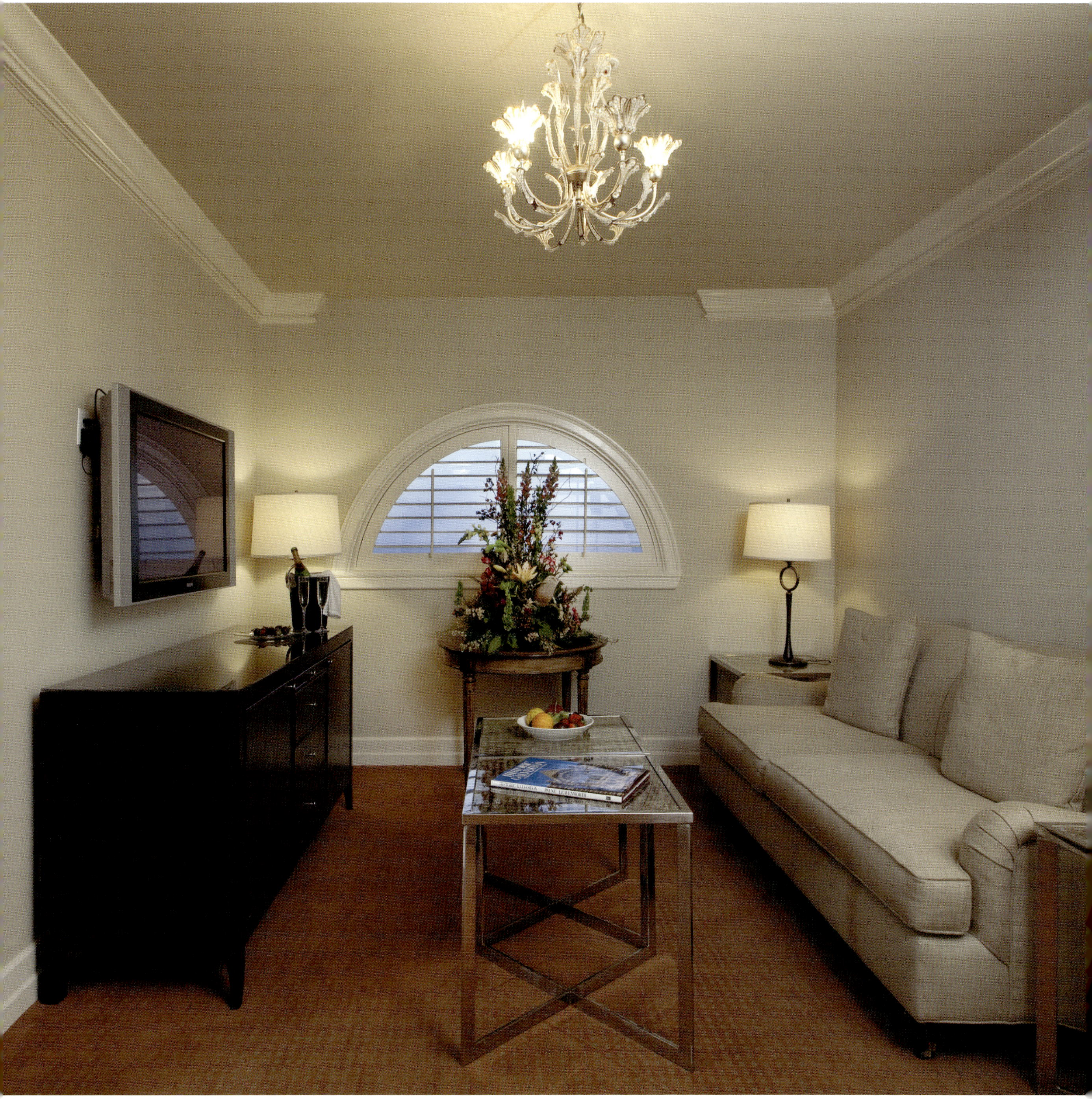

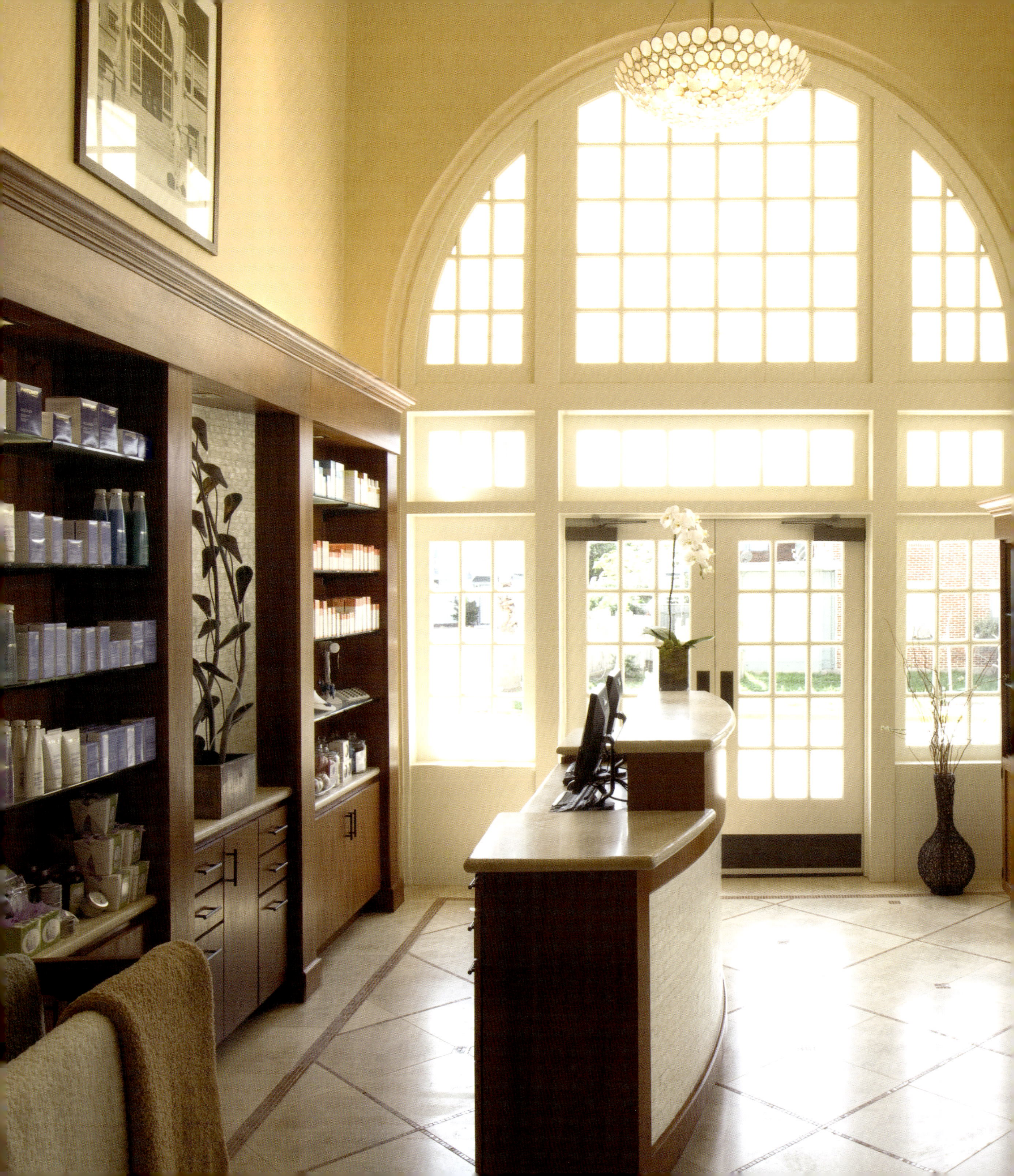

The new Spa at the Hotel Galvez, opened in March 2008, occupies a good portion of the building's lower level. In some ways this nearly ten thousand-square-foot oasis inspired by the sea is a return to the space's original purpose: when the hotel opened, it housed a barbershop where the salon is now, along with a drugstore. The Spa's design team was led by Sheridan Mitchell Lorenz and her niece Lori Sheridan Mitchell, a granddaughter of George and Cynthia Mitchell. This luxurious addition caters to a large number of bridal parties throughout the year, as well as to hotel guests and Galveston residents. As part of the design, an outdoor Meditation Garden was added. Guest rooms on the sixth floor were upgraded by Lori Mitchell to create spa-inspired spaces that offer a soothing ambience with a neutral color palette, luxurious bedding, and rain showers; all are allergy friendly.

Just six months after its opening, the Spa got a genuine, if unwelcome, taste of the sea when Hurricane Ike hit the Island in September 2008 with 110-mile-per-hour winds. The hurricane's storm surge spared the main lobby and other parts of the Galvez, but it deposited nearly two feet of water on the lower-level floor housing the Spa, fitness center, business offices, and laundry room; the roof lost some clay tiles. After the damage was repaired, the Spa at the Hotel Galvez reopened on June 10, 2009—the hotel's ninety-eighth anniversary.

One of the most dramatic changes executed during the Mitchell restoration was the decision to restore the hotel's main entrance to the south side of the hotel, facing the Gulf. That is where its architects intended it to be all along, but over the years other owners had reconfigured the lobby so that the entrance became the porte cochere on the north side, facing in the direction of downtown and the bay rather than the Gulf. To George Mitchell's great credit, the double front door of the hotel again allows visitors a panoramic view of the Gulf of Mexico, the Galvez's *raison d'être*.

Left: The Spa is entered through what was originally the hotel's west entrance, which now opens into a serene reception area naturally lighted by a tall arched window. Above: Spa treatments at the Galvez are inspired by the sea, with hydrotherapy baths, facials, and massages enhanced with marine extracts.

QUEEN OF THE GULF · 47

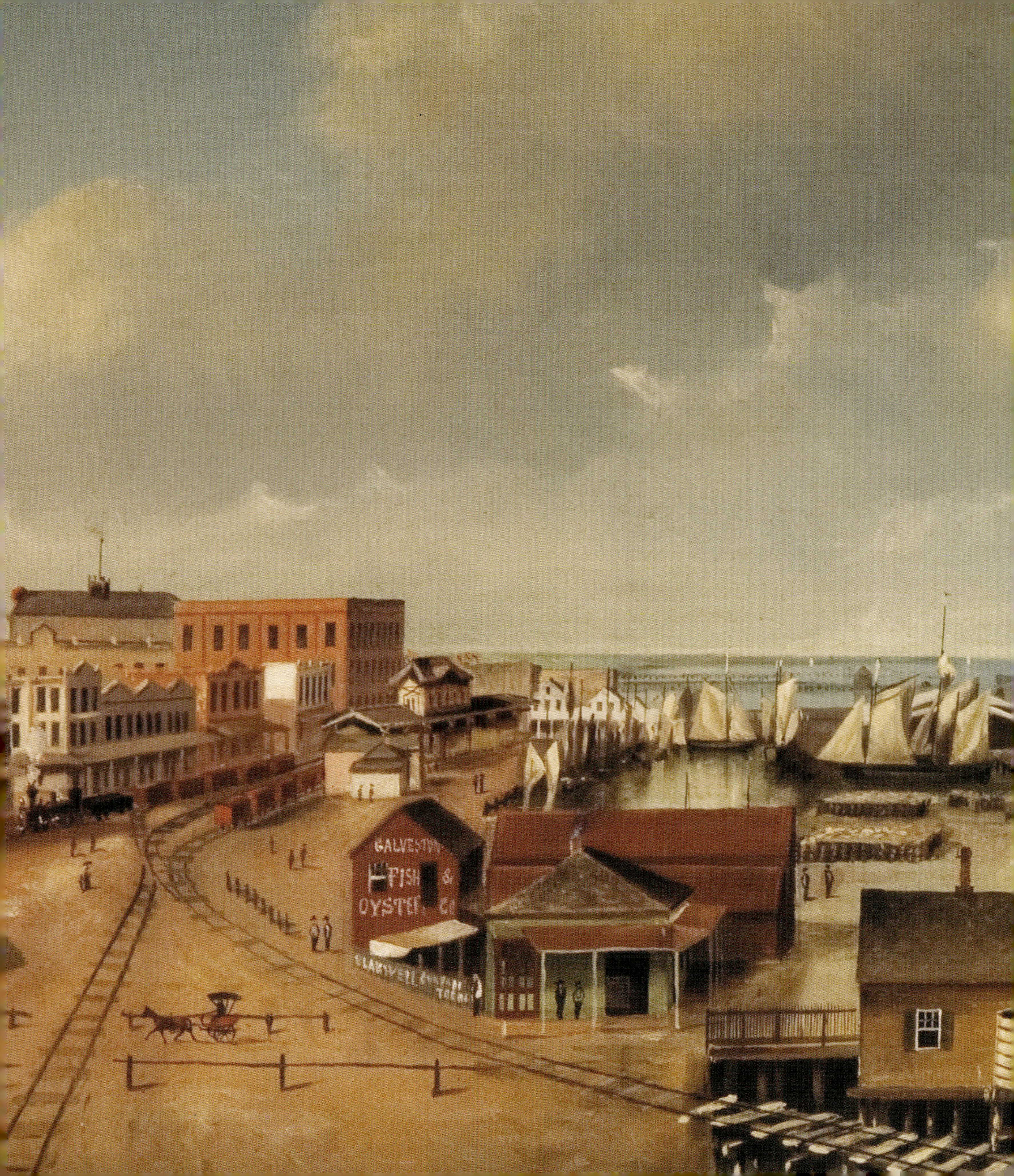
GALVESTON
FISH &
OYSTER CO

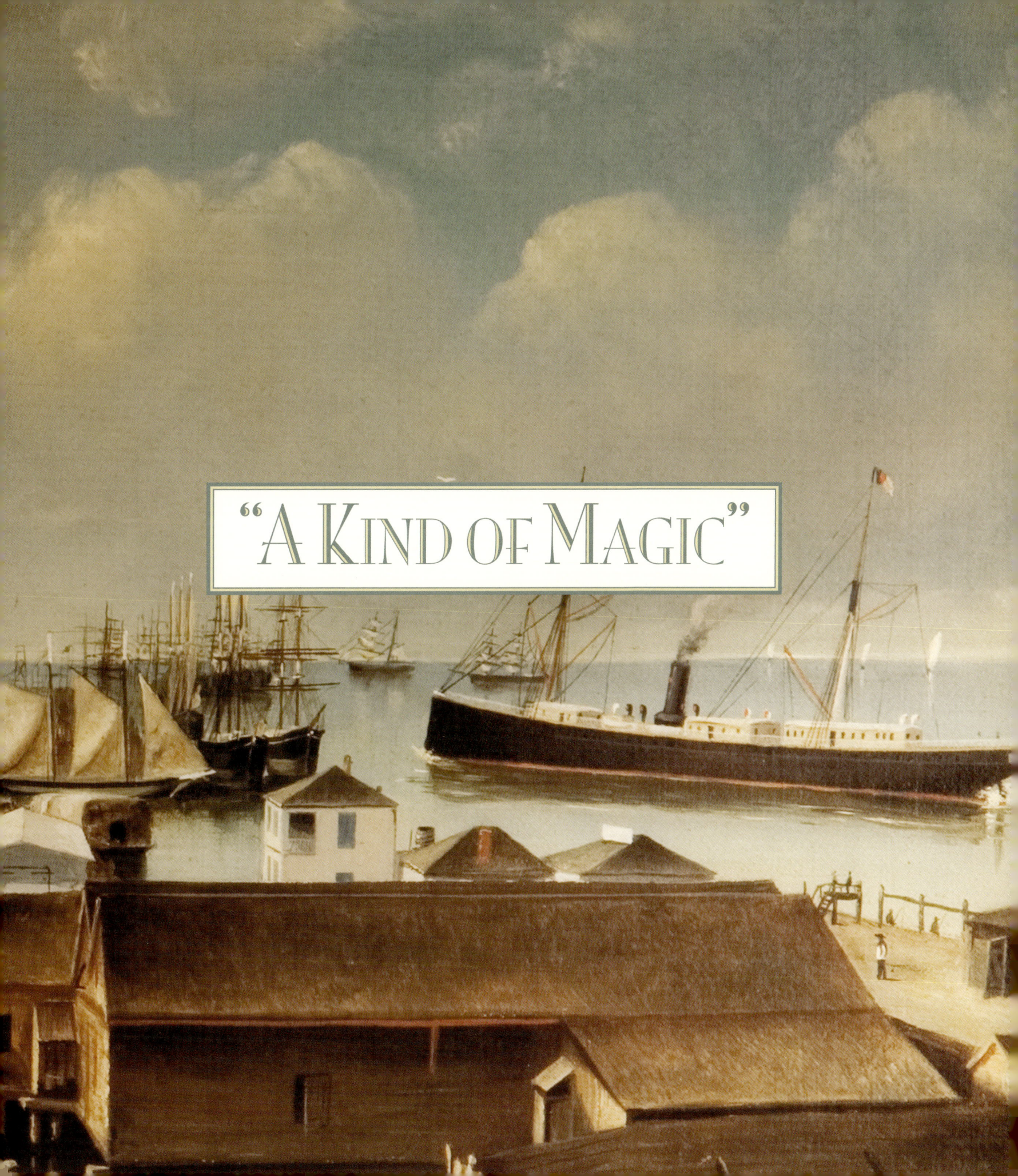

"A Kind of Magic"

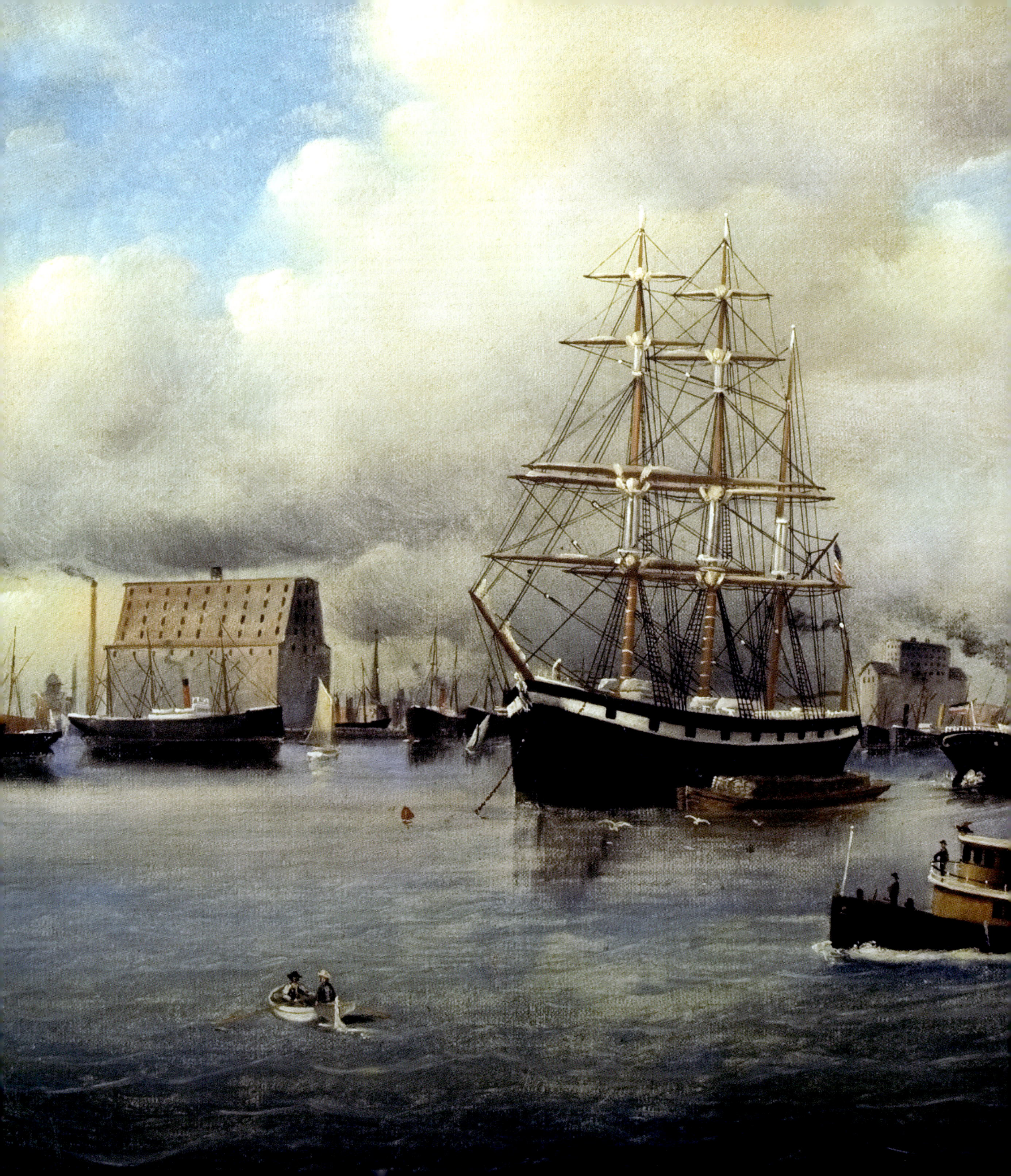

THE FREE STATE OF GALVESTON

More than anything else, the Hotel Galvez and Spa is the living incarnation of Galveston's ghostly charm—a "kind of magic," in the words of Edna Ferber. This barrier island is neck deep in the dust of history and knows exactly how to use what nature and providence provide. In the sixteenth century, it gained the name Malhado (Island of Misfortune), a prescient denomination bestowed by the Spanish explorer Cabeza de Vaca, who endured his own misfortune by being shipwrecked here between 1528 and 1534. Galveston came under the control of the French privateer Jean Laffite from 1817 to 1821. Laffite arrived from New Orleans, renamed the island Campeachy, and made himself "governor." The congress of Mexico, whose flag flew over the Island from 1821 to 1836, turned Galveston into a provisional port. When Stephen F. Austin visited in 1825, he praised the natural harbor as the best he had ever seen. During the Civil War, both the Union and the Confederacy occupied Galveston, neither army inflicting much pain or damage. On the contrary, while the rest of the country suffered great deprivation, the Island got even richer running the federal blockade.

Left and top: In addition to *Galveston Wharf Scene* (1885), shown on the previous pages, the immigrant German painter Julius Stockfleth (1857–1935) captured Galveston Harbor as part of his artistic record of the Island. Reproductions of all three are displayed behind the front desk. Above: Visitors could tour the harbor from the excursion boat *Galvez*, pictured in a postcard.

Above: Since its opening, The Grand 1894 Opera House has presented the best theatrical productions and entertainers in Texas. Right: One of Galveston's largest Mardi Gras balls is held at The Tremont House. The spectacular Mardi Gras arch here was designed by the San Antonio architect Boone Powell.

Galveston had a way of inventing and then reinventing itself. Once seen as a utilitarian barrier from the ravages of the sea, Seawall Boulevard, begun in 1902, now seems born to be one of the world's great marine drives. Stars such as Al Jolson, Sarah Bernhardt, and the great Russian ballerina Anna Pavlova performed on the stage of The Grand 1894 Opera House, which was modeled after the grand opera houses of Europe—and on its scale was the equal to any of them. Lost for many years behind weathered, wooden facades, virtually forgotten, the opera house was rediscovered and restored to its original elegance in the 1980s. It stands today, designated as the "Official Opera House of Texas," just a short distance from the Galvez.

A block from the bay is the famous Strand, with its rows of spectacular Victorian buildings. Home to bankers and wheeler-dealers, The Strand was once known as the Wall Street of the Southwest. There was always a feeling of royalty on the Island, a belief that the great ships that came and went carried with them the entitlements of aristocracy, although in fact most of them were loaded with immigrants and refugees from Eastern Europe and Russia. The Island owes its uniqueness not to royal heritage but to the experiences and diversity of the hundreds of Poles, Czechs, Swedes, French, Italians, Serbs, Croatians, Greeks, Russians, and a wide variety of Asians who found their way to these shores and made Galveston their own. Jewish families arrived when the Port of New York City became overcrowded; some moved on to other Texas cities, but many stayed. The immigrant neighborhood where George Mitchell grew up, for example, was known as the League of Nations.

THE TREMONT HOUSE

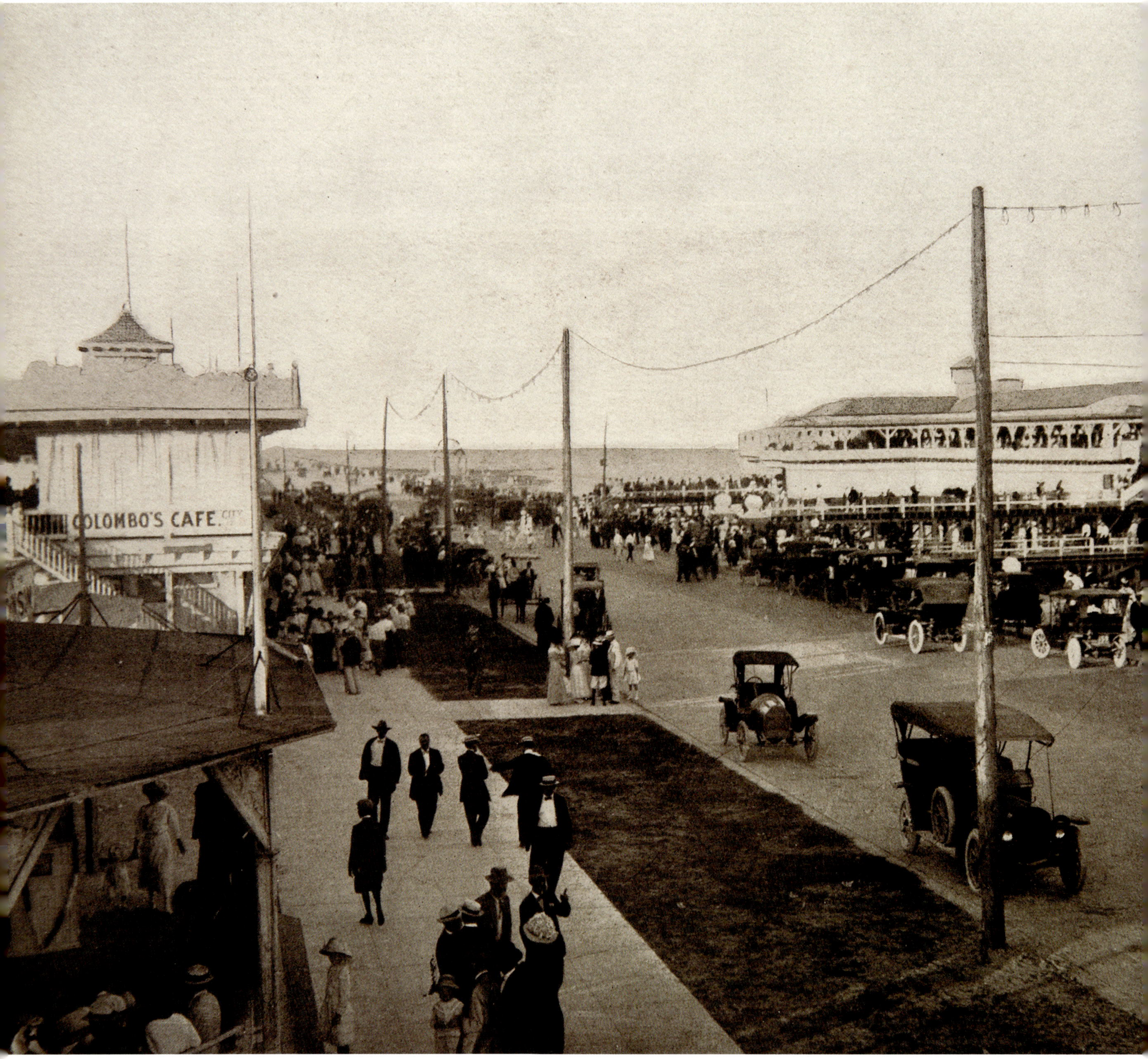
COLOMBO'S CAFE.

In the years between the end of the Civil War and the start of the twentieth century, Galveston was the largest, bawdiest, and most important city between New Orleans and San Francisco, the undisputed gateway to Texas, and the second richest city in America. Fancy shops sold fine English carpets, French china, wine, brandy, and German-made rosewood pianos. In 1858 alone, Islanders purchased twenty-three grand pianos. Galveston had the first gaslight, the first electric light, the first telephone, the first hospital, the first law firm, the first trade union, the first golf course—name any business, institution, or invention, and Galveston had the first in Texas.

During the Island's heyday from 1920 until the 1960s, Seawall Boulevard was a glittering strip of casinos, nightclubs, and pleasure piers. The Balinese Room hosted the biggest names in show business—Frank Sinatra, Frankie Laine, the Marx Brothers, Jayne Mansfield, Bob Hope, the list seemed endless—not to mention the highest-rolling gamblers, including the Houston oilmen Diamond Jim West, Glenn McCarthy, and Jack Josey. These players gambled for stakes approaching the national debt. Situated on the T-head at the end of a long pier, the B-Room was a brassy metaphor for what was called at the time the Free State of Galveston. Like the Island's gambling fever, the Balinese is long gone now, wrecked by a series of hurricanes and by axe-wielding Texas Rangers who finally made it past the front-door security. In 2002 a Houston investor spent about a half million dollars renovating and reopening the Balinese—without the gambling or the top-drawer entertainment, of course—but his good work was completely undone by Hurricane Ike in September 2008. What remains of the Balinese is still visible from the front lawn of the Galvez: the splintered stubs of seven piers, each occupied on most days by a single pelican.

Opposite: With its cafes, bathhouses, and amusement parks, Galveston's Seawall Boulevard, seen in 1911 looking east, has attracted visitors for more than a century. Above: During the 1910s and early 1920s, automobile races were held regularly on the beach. Top right: A postcard documents the notorious Balinese Room, which was one of the Maceo clubs that formed the oddly named Turf Athletic Club. Bottom right: An unidentified chanteuse and her accompanist entertain Balinese Room patrons during the 1940s.

"A KIND OF MAGIC" · 55

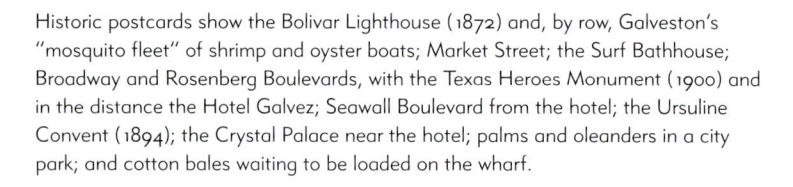

Historic postcards show the Bolivar Lighthouse (1872) and, by row, Galveston's "mosquito fleet" of shrimp and oyster boats; Market Street; the Surf Bathhouse; Broadway and Rosenberg Boulevards, with the Texas Heroes Monument (1900) and in the distance the Hotel Galvez; Seawall Boulevard from the hotel; the Ursuline Convent (1894); the Crystal Palace near the hotel; palms and oleanders in a city park; and cotton bales waiting to be loaded on the wharf.

- 7317. Market Street, Looking West, Galveston, Tex.
- 8365. Surf Bathing Pavilion, Galveston, Texas.
- A BEACH SCENE — GALVESTON, TEXAS
- 7323. Ursline Convent, Galveston, Tex.
- 7324. Palms and Oleanders in City Park, Galveston, Tex.
- 7320. Loading Cotton, Galveston, Tex.

The Great Storm

Hurricanes have traditionally defined Galveston, ushering in changes of direction if not attitude. The Galvez owes its existence to two Island tragedies: the 1900 storm and the fire that swept through the Beach Hotel two years before that. The Beach Hotel (1883) was an Island landmark, a dazzling two hundred-room, three-story Victorian structure designed by the famed Galveston architect Nicholas Clayton (1840–1916). It sat squarely on the beach, at the foot of Twenty-third Street, about where the most recent incarnation of Murdoch's Pier now sits. Almost from the moment the Beach Hotel burned in 1898, leading citizens, in particular Ike Kempner, a banker who was elected city treasurer in 1899, started talking about the need for a new world-class resort hotel near the beach and about an even more urgent need to build a seawall to spare the city the ravages of future hurricanes. Unfortunately, that is all it was—talk. Then the 1900 storm changed everything.

The hurricane struck without warning, in an era when the U.S. Weather Bureau's Galveston Station consisted of two brothers, Isaac and Joseph Cline. They recognized the signs of trouble: a falling barometer and a tide that was rising even though the wind was blowing directly against it. The phenomenon of high water with opposing wind signaled the coming of what was called a storm tide. But there was little time to warn people, and Galvestonians had lived through hurricanes before and tended to disregard the dangers.

But this storm was something else. The rain started just after midnight on Friday, September 7, and by Saturday morning water was running waist deep in the streets. North winds were driving angry waves over the wharves. The wagon bridge and the three railroad bridges across the bay were already under water, meaning that it was too late to escape. Soon the wind was gusting at 120 miles per hour. Houses and railroad trestles were being ripped to splinters, creating a giant ball of debris that trundled across the Island, crushing everything and everyone in its path.

By Sunday morning the storm was gone, but what remained was a scene out of hell. Naked, mutilated corpses were heaped together in the streets or buried under debris as high as four-story buildings. The homeless, a category that included almost everyone still alive, took refuge anywhere they could—in the train station, at city hall, in commercial buildings, warehouses, and the private homes that were still standing. In the week that followed, carts and wagons full of corpses plodded along the ravaged streets toward the wharves, where the bodies were loaded into barges for burial at sea. A few days later, to everyone's horror, the bodies began to wash back on the beach. Eventually the corpses had to be burned, in a series of gigantic bonfires that could be seen from the mainland. People never forgot the smell of burning bodies or the horror of that night.

Top: The Beach Hotel (1883), on the Gulf at Twenty-third Street, was the finest resort hotel on the Texas coast before it was lost to fire in 1898. Above: The Great Storm of 1900 destroyed a large section of the city and twisted some houses beyond repair. It remains the greatest natural disaster ever to strike the United States. Opposite: Survivors cleared a passageway through the debris on Nineteenth Street.

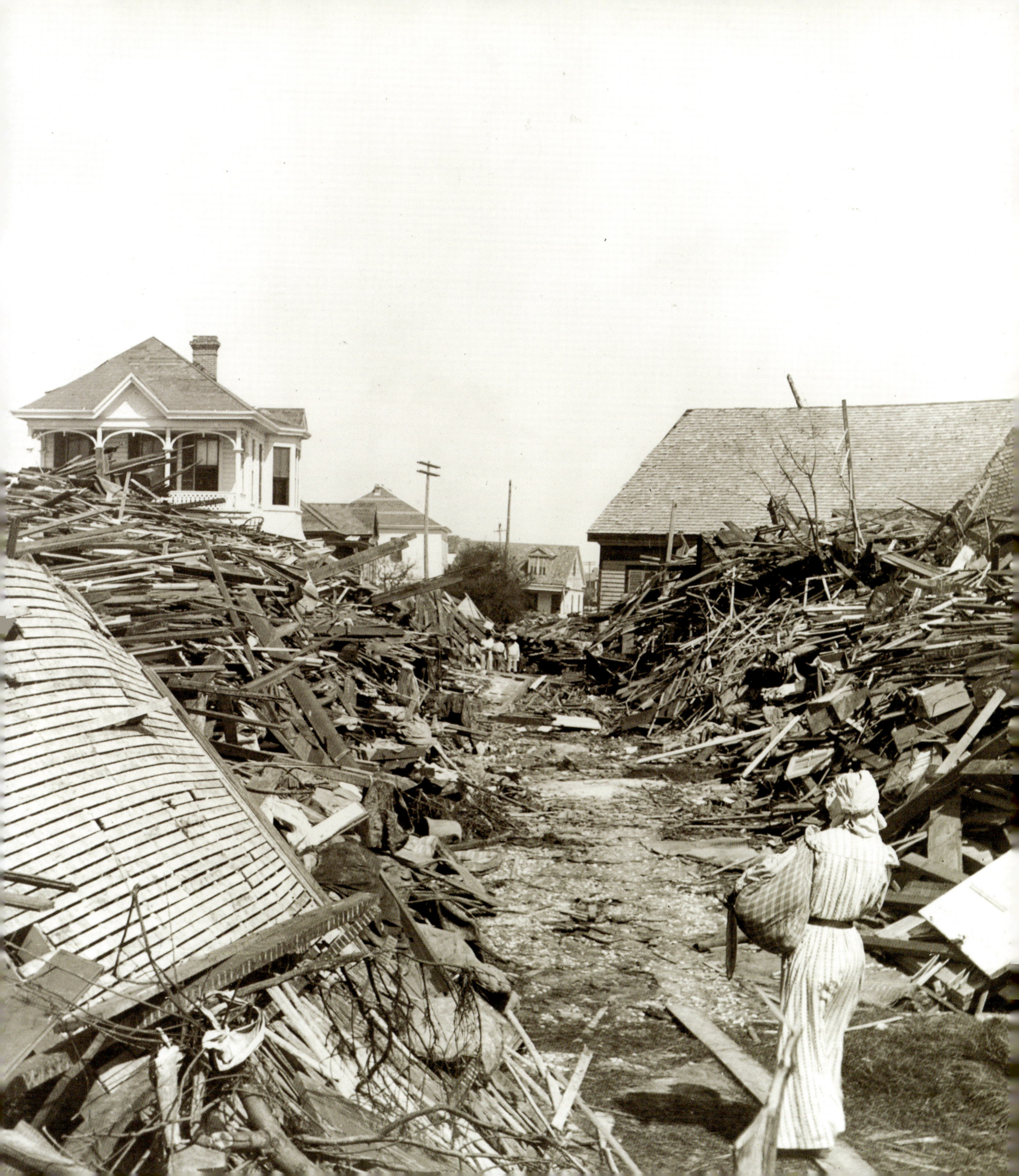

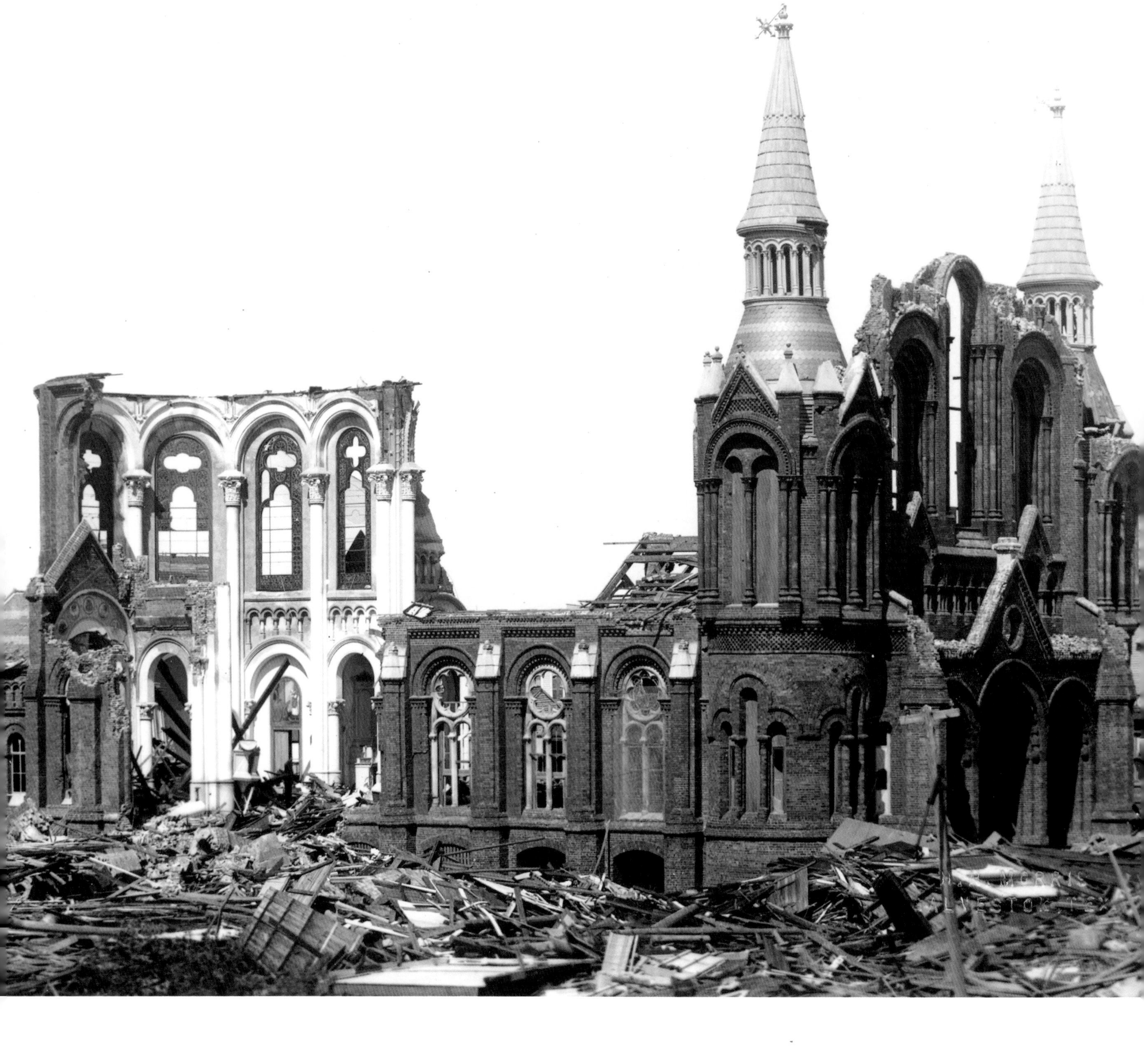
MORRIS

Opposite: The 1900 hurricane destroyed such Galveston landmarks as the Sacred Heart Catholic Church. Above and right: Construction of the seawall began in 1903, with alternating concrete sections poured and gaps filled in later.

Many predicted that the city of Galveston would never be rebuilt, at least on the Island. But mainlanders failed to reckon with the Islanders' tenacity. Literally lifting themselves up by their own bootstraps, starting in 1902, the people of Galveston built a seawall seventeen feet tall and three miles long. It was one of the great engineering feats of the twentieth century, right up there with the Panama Canal and Hoover Dam. Over the years the seawall was extended, until by 1960 it was 10.4 miles long and girded one-third of the Island's coastline.

But constructing the seawall was child's play compared to the task that followed: raising the entire elevation of the city. Houses, churches, and schools alike were raised on jackscrews and filled in with sand underneath. Streetcar tracks, water pipes, gas lines, trees, even cemeteries had to be elevated. Near the seawall the grade was raised about seven feet, the level tapering off inland. It took seven hundred jackscrews to lift the newly restored three thousand-ton St. Patrick's Church a mere five feet, and it was accomplished without interrupting services.

For six of the weirdest years in Galveston's history, monster-size seagoing dredges imported from Germany—some so large that they had to be moved by tugboat—puffed along canals dug across the city, delivering sand dredged from the ship channel. The canals had been excavated for this precise purpose and became part of the scenery; for years Galveston looked like a river town, with people walking across planks or trestles or drawbridges, living with mud and unbelievable inconvenience. Galveston's famed threshold of tolerance was put to the test many times. When two giant dredges collided and sank at Seventh Street and Avenue K, people brought picnic lunches and waited to see what the engineers would do next.

"A KIND OF MAGIC" · 61

Picking Up the Pieces

Undaunted by the chaos, a group of Galveston businessmen got together in February 1910 to begin discussing plans to build a new hotel. This new hotel was meant to be a grandiose structure, one that an issue of *Hotel World* later predicted (in October 1910) would "make Galveston the Atlantic City of the South." The founding investors, who called themselves the Galveston Hotel Company, included the local bankers Ike Kempner, Bertrand Adoue, and John Sealy, as well as H. S. Cooper of the Galveston Electric Company, each of whom put up $50,000 seed money. "What is absolutely essential," the Galveston Hotel Company proclaimed, "is a generous co-operation, a revival of the spirit of 1902, when, sorely afflicted in mind, in body and in purse, the citizens of Galveston challenged universal admiration by subscribing to the Seawall bonds." Public subscription for the new hotel eventually swelled the fund to nearly $1 million, a staggering sum for its day.

There was considerable debate on what to call the hotel. The Dixie Hotel was suggested and then rejected as too regional, as well as associated too closely with advertising schemes that had cheapened a once-proud identity. The Galveston Beach Hotel was also rejected because it implied that this was merely a summer resort—a hotel, like the old Beach Hotel, that would close during the winter. Besides, the new hotel was not actually on the beach, but across the boulevard. Members of the Galveston Hotel Company eventually compromised on the name Hotel Galvez and promoted it as a year-round resort hotel.

The group of founding investors was remarkable not for who came to the table but for who did not. At the time three elite families dominated the social and economic fortunes of Galveston: the Sealys, the Kempners, and the Moodys. Of this elite group, only the Moodys were absent among the Galvez investors. There was no love lost among any of these three families, nor could they have been less alike. The Sealys were patricians and aristocrats, descended from Le Sire de Caillia (or Cely), who had accompanied William the Conqueror to England during the Norman invasion. The Kempner patriarch, Harris Kempner, left Poland at the age of sixteen and arrived in New York, where he worked as a day laborer and studied English at night. After his service in the Confederate Army, he moved to Galveston and founded a mercantile enterprise. Col. William Lewis Moody made his name as a Confederate officer during the Civil War and his fortune in the postwar years, partly by controlling the price of cotton in Texas.

The Moodys believed that the proper business of Galveston was cotton and shipping, not tourism. W. L. Moody Jr., the colonel's son and heir, eventually started his own chain of hotels, the National Hotel Corporation. In 1940 Moody's company, acting through a third party, bought the Galvez from the Galveston Hotel Company, prevailing after all.

Top: The new seawall gave the Island a grand Seawall Boulevard.
Above: Murdoch's Bathhouse occupied a section along the seawall, shown before the Galvez was constructed. Opposite, left to right: Hotel principals included Ike Kempner, Bertrand Adoue, John Sealy, and later owner W. L. Moody Jr.

BOULEVARD HOTEL
BEACH HOTEL
The Haines Photo Co.
Conneaut, O.

The Haines Photo Co.
Conneaut, O.

HOTEL GALVEZ
NEW MILLION DOLLAR FIREPROOF HOTEL
OPEN SPRING 1911.

A Landmark Rises

For reasons lost to history, the founding group decided not to hire Galveston's most famous architect, Nicholas Clayton, who had been lured to the Island in 1872 by Harris Kempner to supervise construction of the second Tremont House hotel. Nor did they hire the famed New York architect Stanford White, whom the Sealys had commissioned to design Open Gates, the Sealy family mansion on Broadway. Instead they gave the job to a St. Louis firm, Mauran and Russell, which went on to become one of the major firms in that city between the world wars and to design other hotels in Texas, including the famous Rice Hotel (1913) in Houston. The firm's principal, John Mauran (1866–1933), started his career at the historic Boston firm Shepley, Rutan and Coolidge and was named a member of the first U.S. Commission of Fine Arts in 1910; five years later, he was elected president of the American Institute of Architects. The interior design was directed by Daniel P. Ritchey.

For the third time in ten years, heavy construction equipment clogged the streets of Galveston in 1910. Working round the clock, a train of two-mule wagons hauled tons of gravel and huge stacks of fully grown tree trunks (more than six hundred of them) to the construction site. Giant pile drivers pounded the thirty-foot tree trunks into the earth, creating a foundation for the great hotel. The pile drivers were cooled by seawater, supplied from a hose stretched across Seawall Boulevard. To furnish salt water for the hotel's natatorium, two pipes were installed beneath the boulevard.

As contractors drilled an artesian well, a rumor circulated that the water would be brackish and undrinkable. One of the Galveston Hotel Company directors, Bertrand Adoue, was quick to brand the rumor false. Putting on his best public relations face, Adoue assured everyone that "as a matter of fact, the water . . . has an actual medicinal value. It has cured me of digestive trouble. The water has a pleasant mineral tinge, very similar to some of the spas at Saratoga (N.Y.)." As it turned out, there was nothing to worry about. At a depth of 950 feet, drillers tapped into an endless supply of clear, fresh water.

As the hotel was being built, construction of the Houston-Galveston Interurban Railroad was nearing completion. The Stone-Webster Syndicate, which had the contract to build the Interurban, subscribed another $50,000 to buy Hotel Galvez stock: its representative, M. M. Phinney, predicted that the Interurban, the Galveston causeway, the beach development, and now the Hotel Galvez would "make Galveston the most important city in Texas." So many reservations came in from eager guests that the hotel opened even before it was completely finished.

Opposite: During construction in 1910, pipes deposited sand to raise the hotel site's grade level to that of the seawall. Top: Proud workers pose in front, when the arched windows were only sketched in. Left: In 1911 Frisco Lines trains brought Midwest vacationers to enjoy Galveston's beaches and hotels.

"A KIND OF MAGIC" · 65

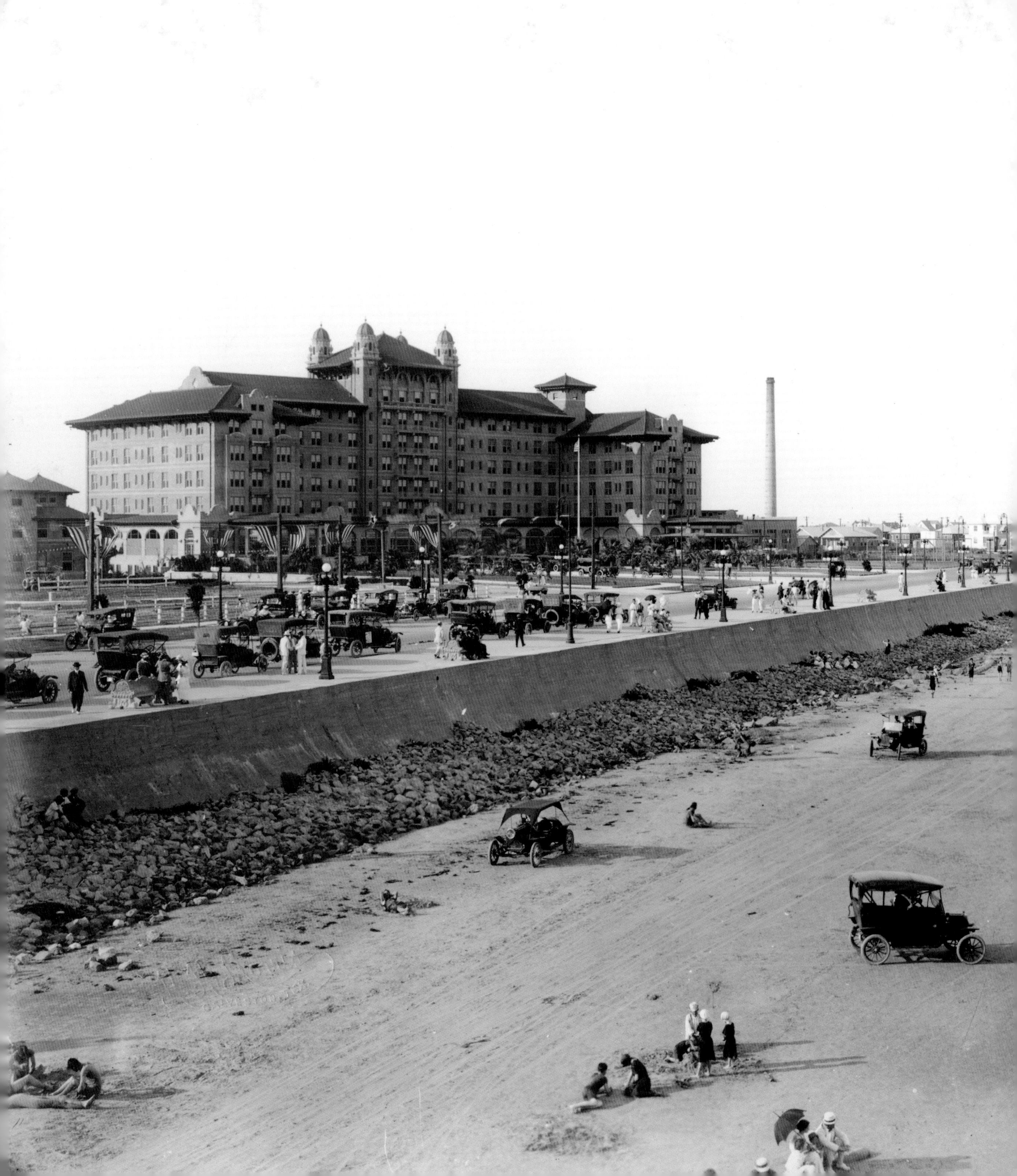

THE GRAND SYMBOL

The Galvez became the Island's grand symbol of survival, an institution that signaled that Galveston was bigger, busier, richer, and more full of life than it had been before the storm. Waiters, imported from New York, arrived en masse, aboard the Mallory Line steamship *Brazos*. Silver service was custom designed. So was the hotel kitchen. No other kitchen in Texas had so many "scientific" do-dads. Potatoes, for example, were pared by an electrically controlled machine that "removed the natural clothing ... at a rate of one bushel in fifty seconds." Another electrically run machine created ice cream. Dishes were washed by an apparatus of complex design and heated in a special compartment. In the basement was a motor-driven printing press where daily menus were churned out and a special hotel newspaper printed. A thirty-two-foot-long ice maker cut blocks of ice into cubes, and a concrete cellar held the hotel's wine. A roller-chair company was formed to manufacture single and double roller chairs with silk sunshades, designed to transport guests along the boulevard.

Left: Vacationers and Galvestonians enjoy late afternoon strolls on the seawall and the broad stretch of beach in front of the Galvez. Above: An arched porte cochere marking the hotel's north entrance hints at the distinctive architectural motif found inside, in the hotel's arched windows and interior arcades.

"A KIND OF MAGIC"

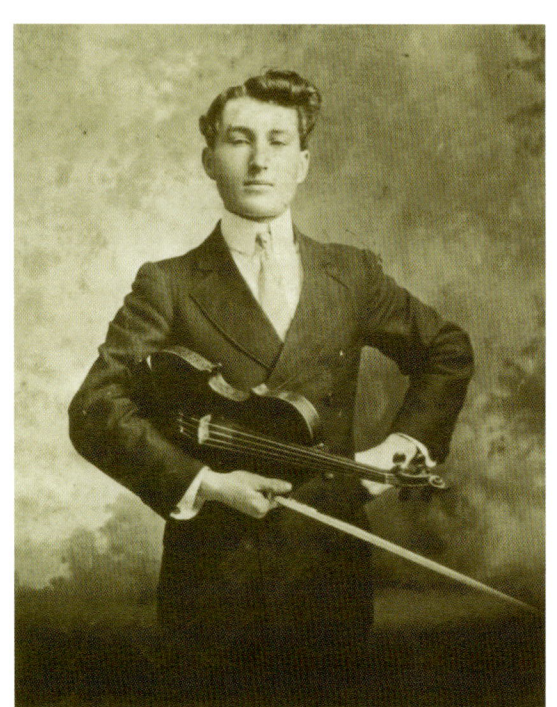

Miss Davis
to meet
Miss Moody
Miss Anne Minor Miss Janet Ferrier
Hotel Galvez
Saturday, the thirteenth of January
Nineteen hundred and twelve

Four to six					R.S.V.P. 1124, 24th Street

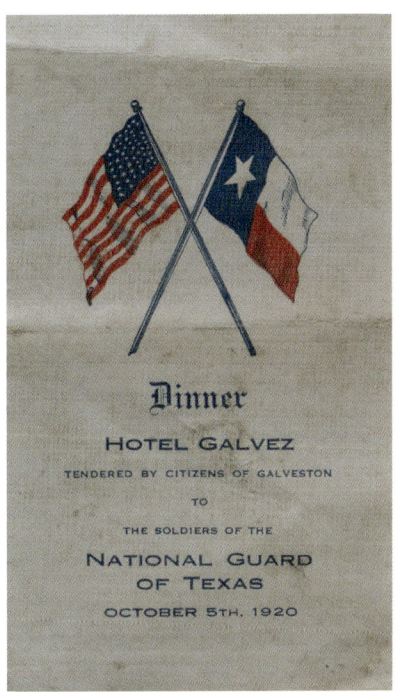

On the eve of the hotel's grand opening, three battleships called on the Port of Galveston: the *Mississippi*, the *Vermont*, and the *Minnesota*. Two days later, army and navy officers in full-dress uniforms were guests of honor at a banquet at the Galvez. The menu was off the charts: Buffet *à la Russe*, Royal Jumbo Squab *au Cresson*, Potatoes Sarah Bernhardt, Salad à la Galvez, Army and Navy Ice Cream. In the east wing, the Second Regiment Coast Artillery Band played "Home Sweet Home" and other toe tappers until the wee hours.

In the days and weeks that followed, the Galvez was the scene of dozens of galas and events celebrating a variety of causes and holidays, from the Galveston Artillery Club Ball and a meeting of the Galveston Equal Suffrage Association to a Halloween dinner dance during which the Galvez presented a silver loving cup to the winner of a dance contest. On New Year's Eve, four hundred guests jammed into the east wing of the Galvez and danced to the music of the Royal Hungarian Court Orchestra. At the stroke of midnight, a giant American flag that had hung from the balcony was hoisted away to reveal a display of electric lights spelling out 1912.

Top left: In the 1920s visitors massed outside the hotel on July 4 to observe a military regiment receiving the colors. Top right: A promotional Galveston postcard featured the Galvez as a backdrop for a bathing beauty. Far left: Joseph Joachim Miller played in the first Hotel Galvez orchestra. Center: Hotel mementoes include an invitation to a 1912 social event, a napkin ring, a Hotel Galvez souvenir cup and saucer, and a dinner program for the National Guard of Texas. Left: David E. Lauber was the hotel's first manager.

"A KIND OF MAGIC" · 69

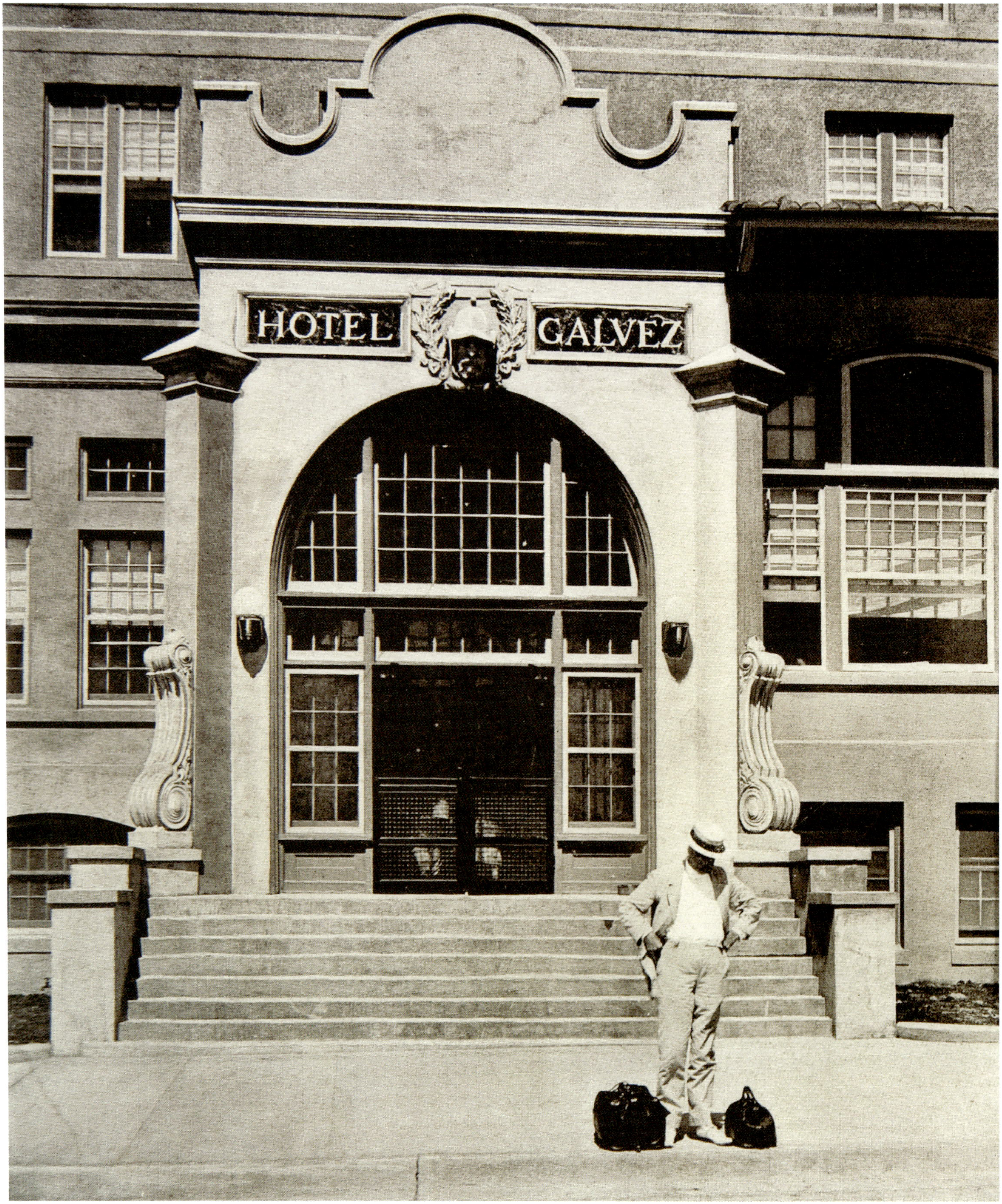
HOTEL
GALVEZ

Opposite: An early Galvez guest waits for a streetcar at the hotel's west entrance on Twenty-first Street. Above: The same entrance now welcomes guests to the luxurious ten thousand-square-foot Spa at the Hotel Galvez.

Hotel Galvez
Galveston, Texas

Opposite top left: A souvenir book featuring gold type on its cover commemorated the opening of the Hotel Galvez in 1911. Top right: The writing room, seen looking through the loggia that same year, provided a quiet retreat for guests to write letters or postcards home. Bottom: The long loggia overlooking the Gulf of Mexico filled the front of the hotel on either side of the lobby. Above: In the west loggia, with its comfortable wicker rockers, arches frame the lobby in the distance. Left: Open to the loggia, a parlor room was available to guests for meeting friends and family.

"A KIND OF MAGIC" · 73

Above: The soda fountain, drugstore, and candy shop were popular attractions when the hotel first welcomed guests in 1911. Right: The barbershop was described in the commemorative booklet as "a modern and sanitary room." Opposite top left: The Marine Dining Room, now Bernardo's restaurant, gained a wall of light from the loggia's arched windows. Top right: The Terrace Restaurant is now the setting for festive social occasions held in the renamed Terrace Ballroom. Bottom: A telescoped view shows three private dining rooms: the Modern Navigation Room, the Ancient Navigation Room, and the Automobile Room, as they appeared in 1911.

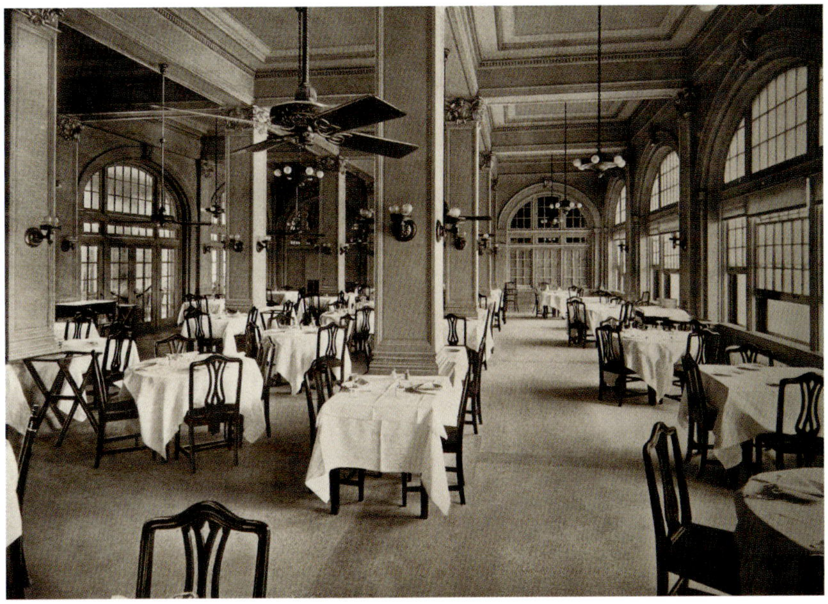

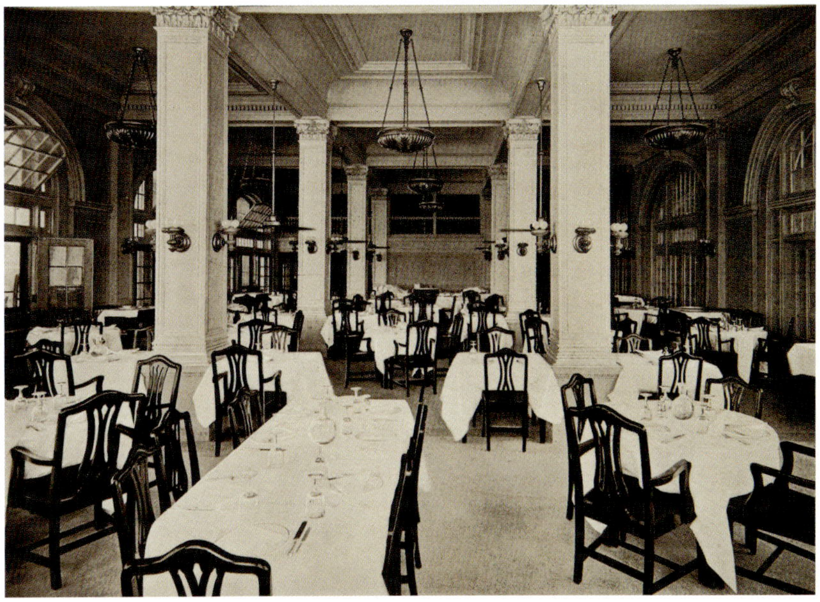

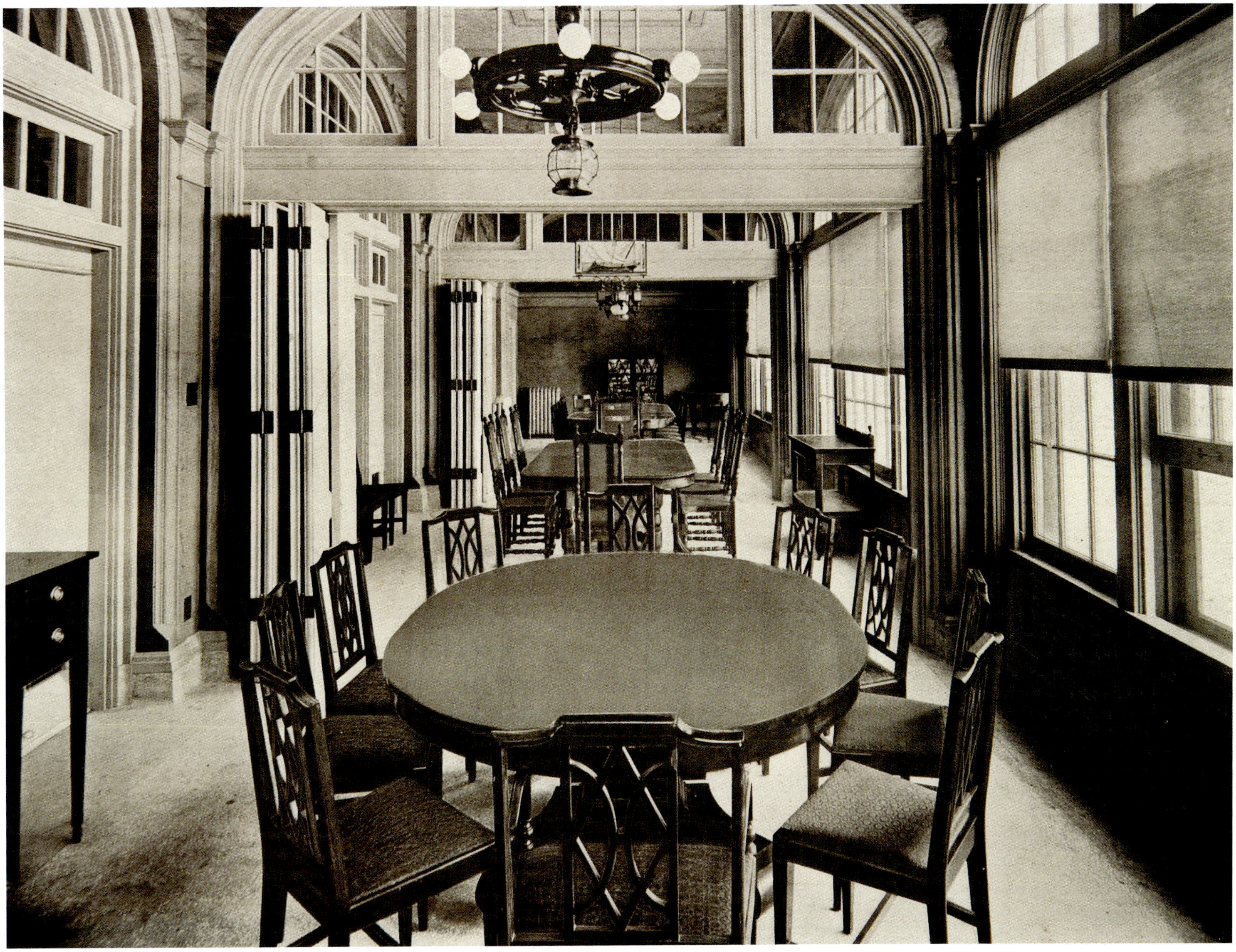

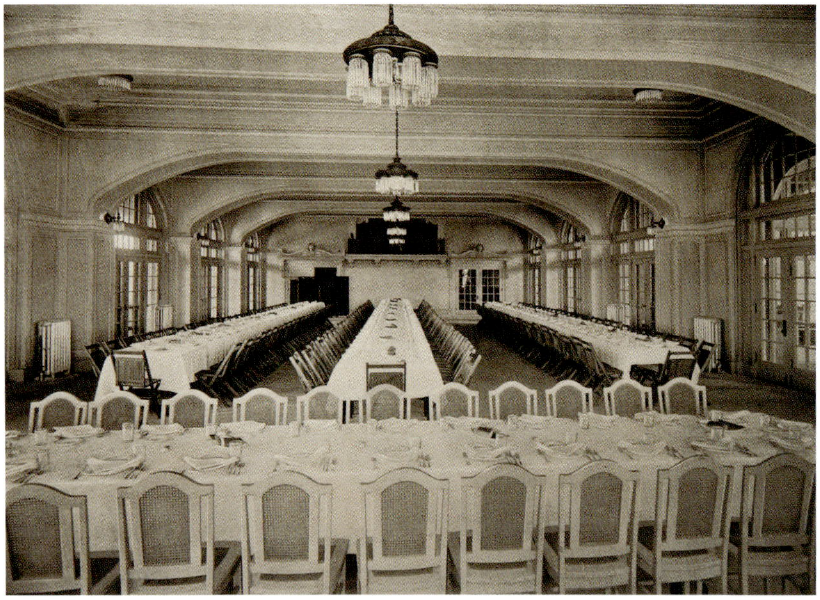
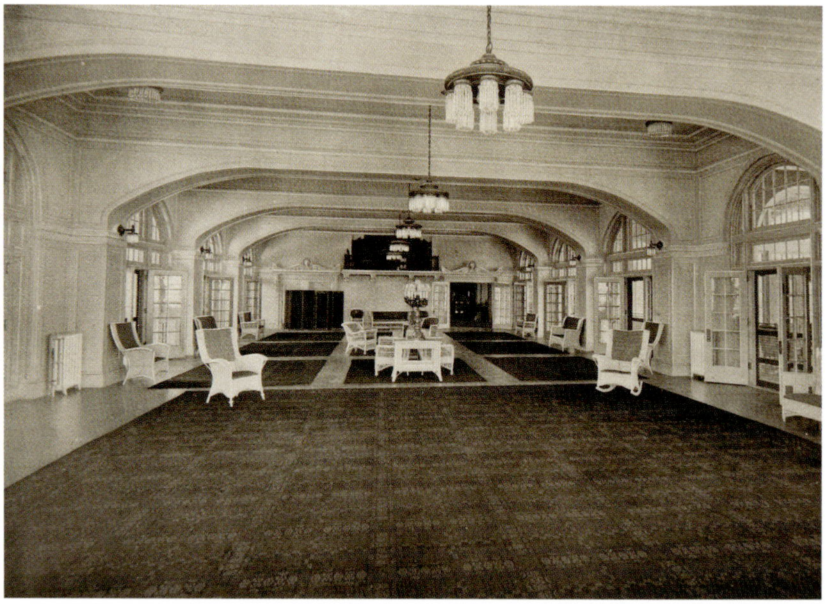
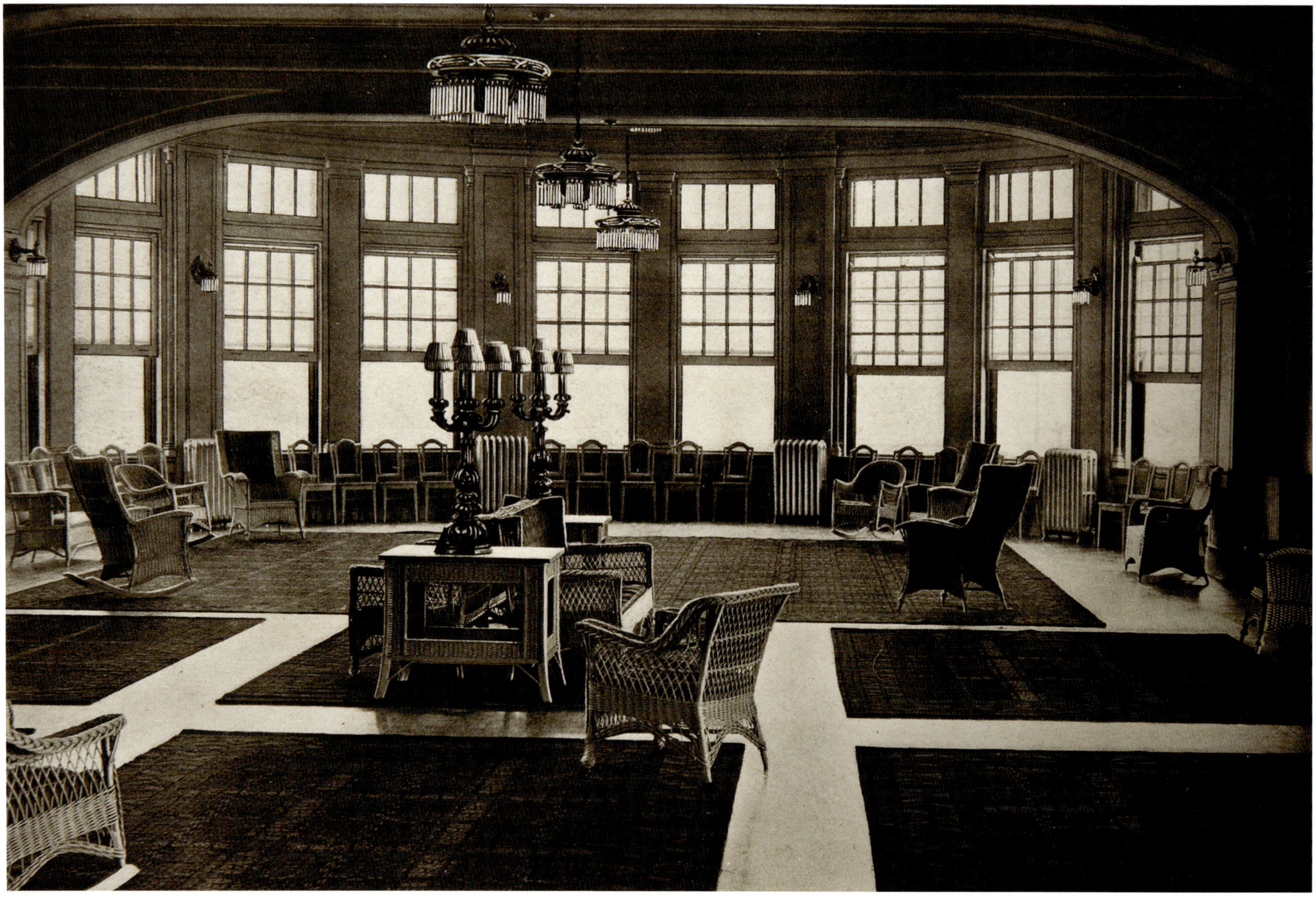

Opposite: Three photographs in the 1911 booklet capture what is now the Music Hall but was also known as the Grecian Room at one point. Since the hotel's opening, the wide-open arches and the room's projecting glass-filled bay have made it an inviting space for special events and meetings. Above: A "typical" early hotel room, according to the publication, had all the amenities a guest would want a century ago. Left: One of the guest suites included this spacious parlor.

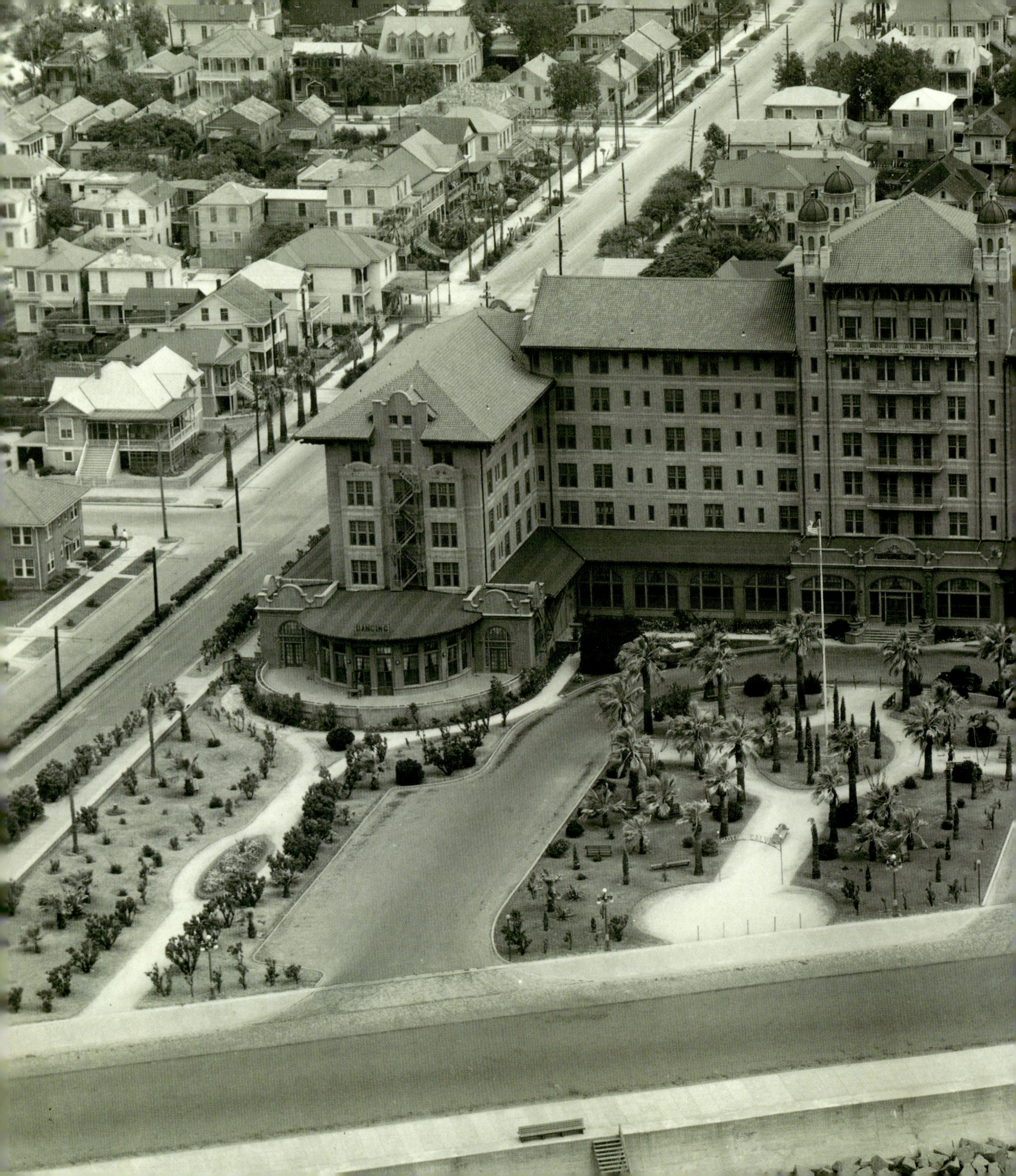
DANCING

America's Treasure Island

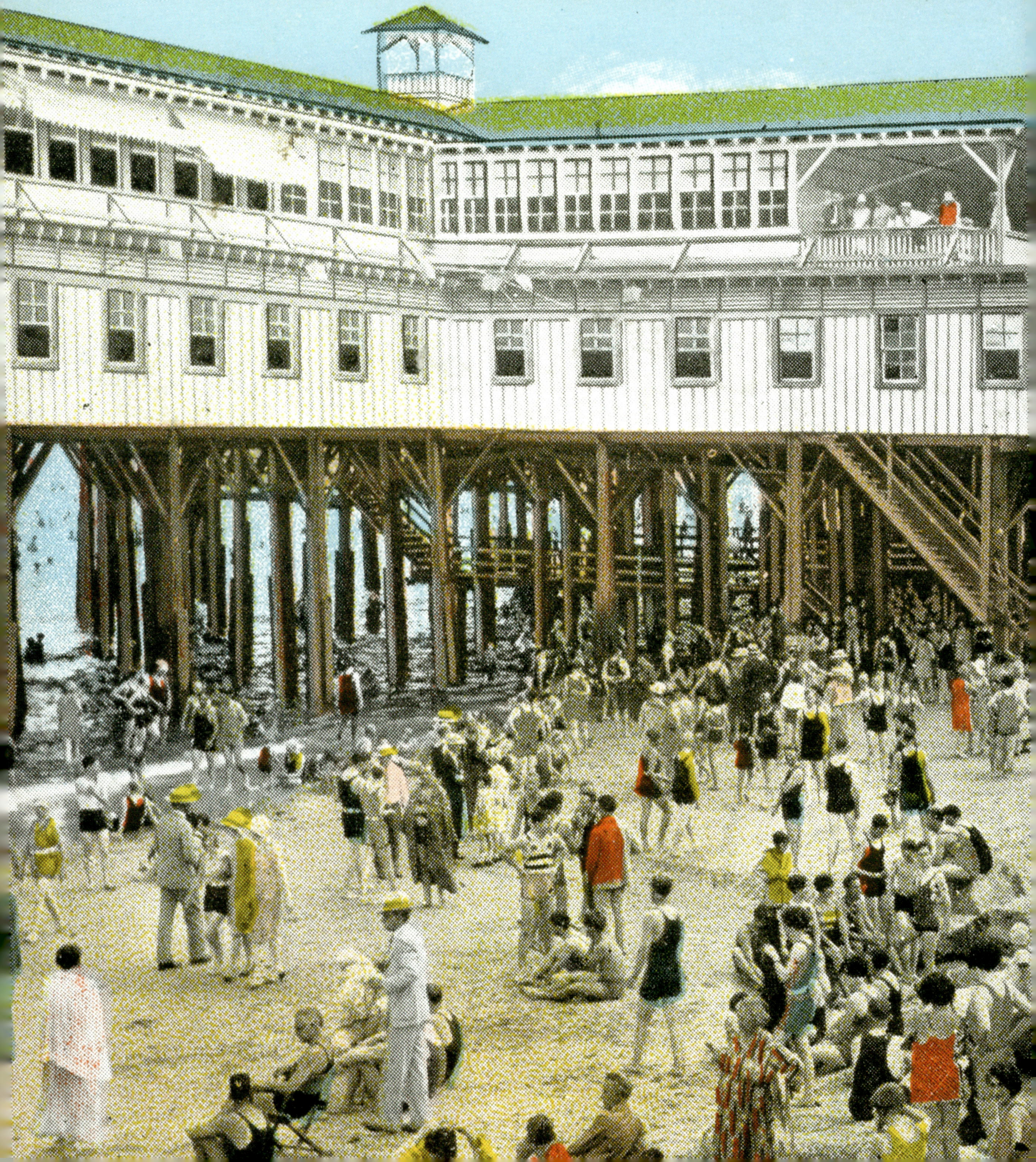

THE GANGS OF GALVESTON

Oceangoing ships were already traveling up the ship channel to Houston by 1914. At the end of World War I, Houston was beginning to nudge aside Galveston as the state's top seaport. Control of the ship channel became a hot-button political issue. Delegates from Houston and Galveston met regularly to debate the problem, often in the lobby of the Galvez and other Island hotels. The debates were noisy and sometimes violent. One became so heated that an official from the Galveston Chamber of Commerce bloodied the nose of his Houston counterpart, who retaliated by smashing the Galvestonian over the head with his cane.

What rescued Galveston's economy was not shipping, however, but something far more elemental—the rackets. While Houston and other cities were feeling the ravages of the Great Depression in the 1930s, Galveston actually began to prosper, thanks to organized crime. Gambling and prostitution had always thrived on the Island, particularly so in times of economic hardship, but the national crisis that really jumpstarted Galveston and kept certain sectors running full throttle for more than forty years was Prohibition, which became the law of the land in January 1920. Galveston had miles of isolated beaches, which made it a perfect venue for smuggling by sea. Schooners from Cuba, Jamaica, and the Bahamas, carrying up to twenty thousand cases at a time, dropped anchor at a rendezvous point thirty-five miles off Galveston's coast—a location known as Rum Row, where the cargo was off-loaded onto launches and delivered to the miles of deserted beach—and thence to Dallas, Houston, Denver, St. Louis, Omaha, and other thirsty cities of the interior.

Like Chicago, Galveston was an immigration center and a breeding ground for gangsters, wise guys impatient for legislatures to think up new crimes to which they could address their talents. Into this land of opportunity drifted two of the best racketeers in Texas history, Rosario "Rose" Maceo and his younger brother, Sam Maceo. Born in Palermo, Sicily, the Maceos migrated with their family to Louisiana about the turn of the century and by 1910 had found their way to Galveston.

The Beach Gang, one of the organized crime groups that kept Galveston afloat during the 1930s, operated out of Murdoch's Pier across Seawall Boulevard from the Galvez. This historic pier began life in the late nineteenth century but has undergone numerous incarnations following storms and changes over several generations of family ownership. An old postcard shows the bustling activity that has long surrounded the pier. In 2008 Hurricane Ike leveled the pier structure, which has since been replaced by yet another version built on the same pilings.

AMERICA'S TREASURE ISLAND · 81

They were barbers by trade. Sam worked in the barbershop on the lower level of the Hotel Galvez, and Rose operated a chair in a corner of a seafood canteen across the street, at Murdoch's Pier, a wide, three-story edifice. Rose sold bottles of liquor concealed in hollowed-out loaves of bread and passed out glasses of "Dago Red" to customers. Almost every cafe, newsstand, and barbershop along Seawall Boulevard sold bootleg booze and had rows of slot machines.

In those days two rival gangs controlled the Island's rackets: the Downtown Gang and the Beach Gang. Broadway was considered the line of demarcation, and the gangs mostly stayed on their own side, avoiding trouble with one another. The Beach Gang worked out of Murdoch's Pier and used a fishing hut on West Beach as a landing spot for illegal shipments. When a shipload of liquor got close to the Island, its captain watched for a flashing light from the roof of the Moody-owned Buccaneer Hotel, a block west of the Galvez: this was a signal that it was safe for boats to land.

The smugglers were always looking for places to stash their cargoes while they awaited transportation to the mainland. Papa Rose was quick to spot this opportunity. He was cutting hair for twenty-five cents and making a little on the side peddling loaves of booze, but he owned a raised beach cottage on West Beach that was a perfect spot to store bottles of whisky. The Maceos bought their way into the rackets and in a few years controlled the entire Island.

Rose was the enforcer, but Sam was the diplomat, gregarious and well mannered, who wore suits custom tailored in New York. He seldom drank, never gambled, and knew how to cultivate celebrities and make them feel at home. A born showman, Big Sam opened a swank nightclub on the western edge of the city, offering gourmet food and a first-class casino. Overnight the Hollywood Dinner Club was the most famous nightspot on the Gulf Coast. Apparently modeled on the Hotel Galvez, the Hollywood featured Spanish architecture, crystal chandeliers, rattan furniture, a dance floor even larger than the Galvez's ballroom, and chilly air conditioning to encourage gambling. A pair of search lights out front made it impossible to miss the Hollywood, and high rollers from all over Texas poured into Galveston to try the action.

For opening night, Sam booked one of the biggest names in the business, Guy Lombardo and his Royal Canadians. They drew twenty thousand customers during their three-night engagement. Sam made it his policy to bring in only the biggest names, such as Ray Noble's band, with Glenn Miller playing first trombone; Sophie Tucker; Joe E. Lewis; the Ritz Brothers. A young hoofer named Fred Astaire signed on as the club's resident dance instructor. The country's first remote radio broadcast originated at the Hollywood, and stars such as the bandleader Phil Harris saw it as a great chance to get national exposure. One night Sam introduced a replacement trumpet player from Beaumont named Harry James. This was all in 1926, years before anyone ever heard of Las Vegas.

Top: Murdoch's Pier grew from a bathing pavilion to include a casino and a restaurant. Above, left to right: Sam Maceo visits with the famous pianist Carmen Cavallero and Galveston Mayor Herbert Y. Cartwright about 1948. Opposite top: The Crystal Palace added its own gambling, dancing, dining, and bathing to the amusements along the boulevard. Bottom left: Rose Maceo and his wife, Frances, on the right, turned out for a 1948 Galveston Mardi Gras dance. Bottom right: Sam Maceo, on the far right, is toasted by friends at the 1947 opening of the Turf Grill.

Coca-Cola
Maxwell
YOUR PHOTO
Coca-Cola
BEN C. DOHERTY & CO.
Satin Oil
BATH HOUSE & PLUNGE
CRYSTAL PALACE
BATHING & AMUSEMENTS

The Maceos soon opened a second big-time dinner club and casino called the Grotto, on a pier off Seawall Boulevard, directly across from the Hotel Galvez. Damaged by a hurricane in 1932, the Grotto reopened later that same year as the Sui Jen and eventually became the Balinese Room. The Maceos formed a new business called the Gulf Vending Company. Soon every barbershop, drugstore, washateria, cafe, and bar on the Island had slot machines, pinball machines, and tip books, supplied by Gulf Vending. "They didn't ask if you wanted their slots," explained Mike Gaido, whose family owned the famous seafood restaurant on Seawall Boulevard. "They just asked how many." Even the Hotel Galvez had its share of slots, which sat near the elevators, about where the front desk is now located.

Money was in the air. Visitors no longer asked about the port or how the cotton market was doing, but about the beach and which casino offered the best odds. For the first time, Galveston was truly a tourist town. Now that the Hollywood Dinner Club had broken the barrier, gambling joints sat on all four corners of Sixty-first Street and Avenue S. The seawall was billed as "Galveston's version of the Atlantic City Boardwalk." Murdoch's Pier expanded to three stories and added a gambling casino, a restaurant, and a bathhouse. Across from the hotel sat the glitzy Crystal Palace, which offered gambling, a dance pavilion, a restaurant, a bathhouse, a penny arcade, and an indoor saltwater swimming pool. A beachside dance pavilion, called the Garden of Tokyo, gave cash prizes to marathon dancers. Above the boulevard at Twenty-fifth Street, the city erected a sixty-foot-high sign in which three thousand electric light bulbs spelled out GALVESTON, THE TREASURE ISLAND OF AMERICA.

A professional showman named Bill Roe was hired to promote the Island's wide-open image and manage its annual bathing revue. Roe transformed the beach area into a perpetual carnival, with a roller coaster and Ferris wheel and games of chance that paid off in hard cash. Roe's bathing-girl revue grew each season and eventually became an extravaganza called the International Pageant of Pulchritude, which in turn evolved into the Miss Universe contest. Contestants arrived from all over the world: in 1929 bathing beauties came from Russia, Romania, Turkey, France, Hungary, England, and a half dozen other countries. The Catholic bishop, Christopher Byrne, preached that the celebration was inspired by the devil and tried his best to have it shut down, but it was too late. The crowd was already 150,000, three times Galveston's population.

Right top: The Pageant of Pulchritude began in 1920, featuring bathing beauties with exotic parasols and attracting huge crowds before it was ended by the Great Depression. Right center: More winsome participants with eye-catching hats appeared in the third annual revue in 1922. Right bottom: A modern-day Bathing Beauty Revue sponsored by Islanders by Choice takes place on the beachfront by the Hotel Galvez each spring. Opposite left: A brilliantly lighted sign welcomed guests to the pleasures of Galveston. Top: Rose and Sam Maceo's Hollywood Dinner Club had seating for five hundred, a large dance floor, thirty dice tables, and other gambling areas. The club closed in 1939 and was destroyed by fire in 1959. Bottom: Phil Harris and his orchestra performed regularly at the Hollywood.

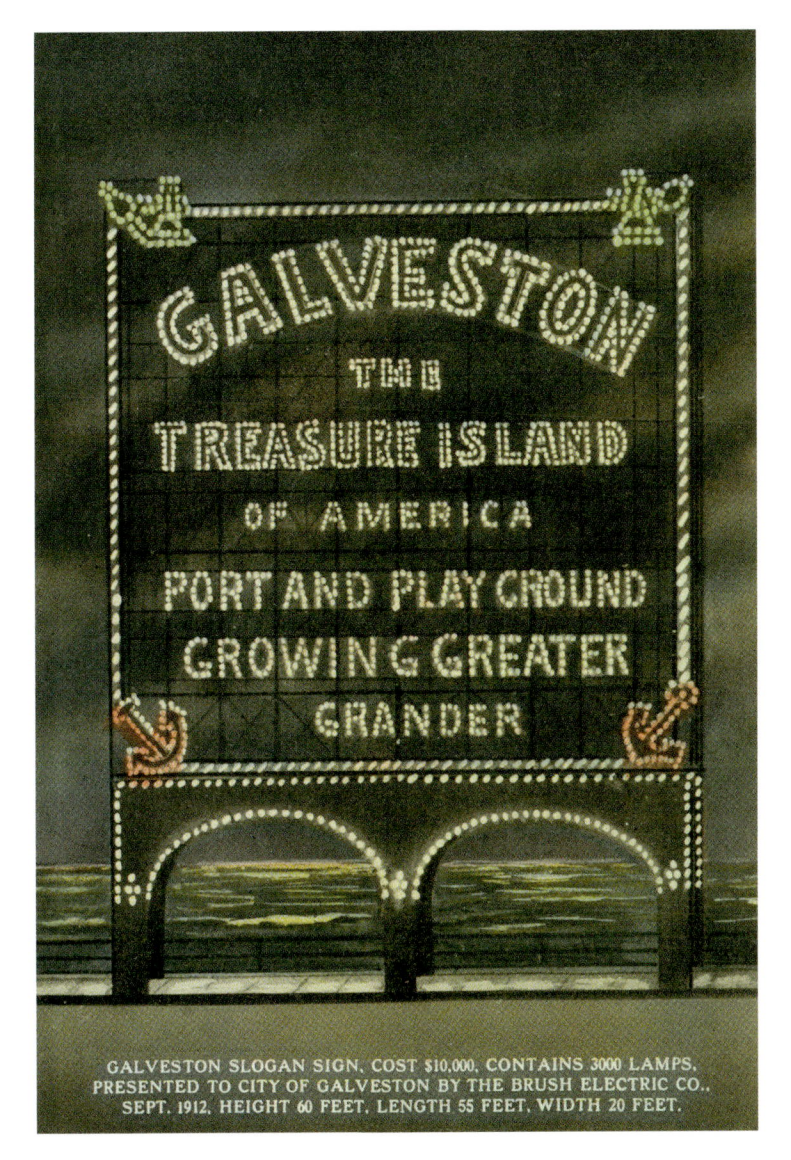

GALVESTON SLOGAN SIGN, COST $10,000, CONTAINS 3000 LAMPS, PRESENTED TO CITY OF GALVESTON BY THE BRUSH ELECTRIC CO., SEPT. 1912, HEIGHT 60 FEET, LENGTH 55 FEET, WIDTH 20 FEET.

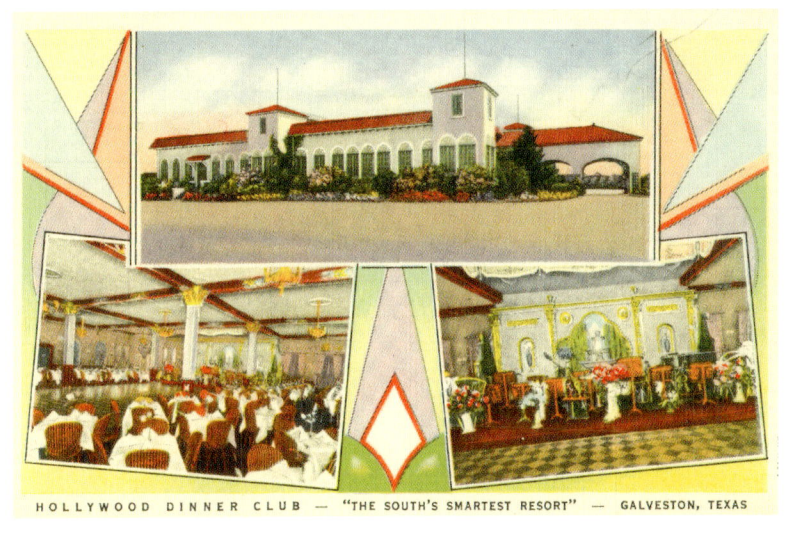

HOLLYWOOD DINNER CLUB — "THE SOUTH'S SMARTEST RESORT" — GALVESTON, TEXAS

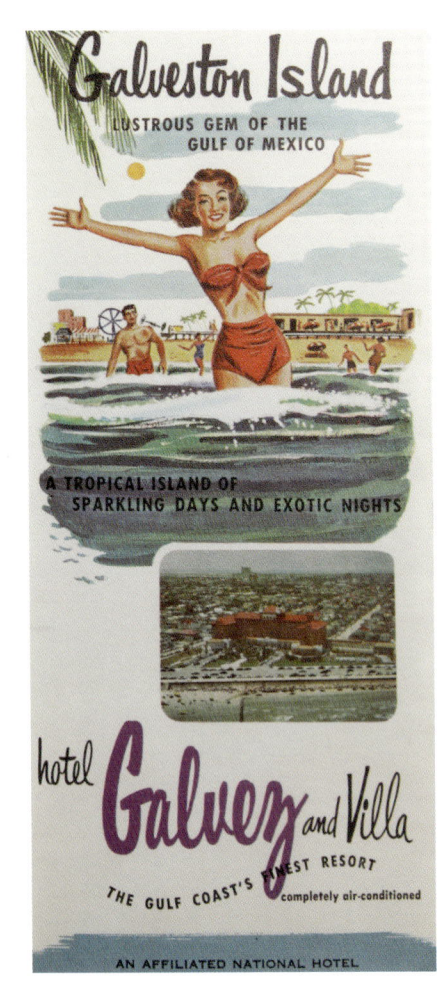

Galveston Island

LUSTROUS GEM OF THE GULF OF MEXICO

A TROPICAL ISLAND OF SPARKLING DAYS AND EXOTIC NIGHTS

hotel Galvez and Villa

THE GULF COAST'S FINEST RESORT — completely air-conditioned

AN AFFILIATED NATIONAL HOTEL

Casual, carefree hours...

VILLA AND POOL

Informality prevails in Galveston... and comfort dictates your attire and activity. So be sure to bring along your swim togs and sports wear, as most of your time will be indolently consumed with luxurious rest and pleasure on the sunny isle. The Galvez's spacious, beautifully landscaped grounds with swaying palms, Hibiscus and abundant flowers and its magnificent swimming pool and beach front location provide an enchanted tropical atmosphere that banishes worry and tension.

Luxurious Suites and guest rooms

■ Your choice of accommodations... if you prefer conventional type rooms, the hotel has spacious stately suites and guest rooms beautifully appointed... or if you lean toward the modernistic, the new Villa features functional studio rooms that serve as living room by day and bedroom at night. ■ Also, Villa guest rooms have private lanai balconies overlooking the Gulf and Galvez pool. ■ Regardless of your preference, both the hotel and Villa offer complete resort hotel services and are equipped with selective television and radios.

COMPLETELY AIR-CONDITIONED — ON THE BEACH
FREE PARKING — DELICIOUS SEAFOOD

GALVEZ BALLROOM *LIVING ROOM*

STUDIO BEDROOM *COFFEE SHOP* *TWIN BEDROOM*

The GALVEZ CLUB

CALENDAR 1952

Galvez Hotel

Galveston, Texas

New Hands on Deck

Shortly before World War II, Sam Maceo led a move to upgrade the Island's tourist facilities and persuaded W. L. Moody III, son of Galveston's most powerful man, to finance a luxury hotel on the east end of the Island. The Jack Tar Hotel was the first Moody-owned hotel to feature air conditioning, but it closed and the son left the Island. After Conrad Hilton defaulted on a partnership with W. L. Moody Jr. in 1927, Moody merged his hotel chain with Hilton's and changed its name to the National Hotel Corporation. The corporation quickly expanded its holdings in Galveston, constructing two new hotels, the Buccaneer and the Jean Laffite.

Moody kept a sharp eye on the Galvez, biding his time. In 1928 the Baker Corporation bought the Galvez from Kempner's group for $1 million. In quick order, the new company began an extensive reconditioning program—new carpets, upgraded furniture, improved plumbing fixtures, including showers in the rooms that did not already have them. In October 1931, using Galveston Mayor Jack E. Pearce as a front, Kempner and his partners quietly repurchased the Galvez. Moody continued to await his moment. In September 1940, as World War II was spreading across Europe, he saw that the time was right. Using an affiliate of the National Hotel Corporation to negotiate a deal, Moody became the sole owner of the Hotel Galvez. It was his crowning moment.

Under Moody's leadership, the Galvez was completely refurbished. The main ballroom was repainted Wedgewood blue, with pale blue ceilings trimmed with Swedish red. The Terrace Room at the east end of the lobby got new Caribbean blue ceilings and walls, white woodwork, gray columns, and new drapes. The kitchen was completely reequipped with stainless steel and new red tile floors. A new swimming pool was constructed on the east lawn, with a system that changed the water every eight hours. The new Galvez Club, open to members only, was constructed in the east wing, spilling out onto the lawn and the pool area.

Moody's most dramatic innovation, however, was the addition of a fifty-one-room ultramodern motel, the Galvez Villa, which he placed on the hotel's east end, in the space once occupied by the Artillery Club. A story in the *Galveston Daily News* reported that "all studio rooms have sliding glass doors which open on private balconies which are identical to the curving lanais of the new Surf Rider Hotel in Honolulu." Many Islanders disliked the addition; it was, as one wag noted, like sticking rabbit ears on the Mona Lisa.

Dear Club Members
Aloha!
May you enjoy our Luau
as much as we have enjoyed
arranging it for you.
Go ahead and have fun!
Sincerely,
Your Club Committee
Galvez Club
Galveston, Texas
July 13, 1958

Opposite top: The Galvez Villa, the midcentury-modern motel added by W. L. Moody Jr., was promoted in colorful brochures such as this in the 1950s. Bottom left: The Villa wrapped around the hotel's new pool along Seawall Boulevard. Left and opposite bottom right: A membership club in the hotel's east wing, "near the pool," sponsored festive get-togethers, including a 1958 luau.

America's Treasure Island · 87

Winds of War

Islanders endured the hardships of World War II with their customary aplomb. Fresh troops were ordered to Fort Crockett, and artillery batteries were planted in giant bunkers near the seawall, where the San Luis Hotel stands today. For the most part, however, Galvestonians continued their live-and-let-live lifestyle. One large exception was the Hotel Galvez, which was drafted into the service of our country. In 1942 the U.S. Coast Guard commandeered the Galvez and made it Coast Guard headquarters. For almost two years, the only guests at the Galvez wore Coast Guard blue.

Rumors of German U-boats prowling the Gulf did not deter entrepreneurs from opening new clubs and casinos. (There was a rumor, never confirmed, that German submariners landed on West Beach one night, enjoyed an evening in Galveston's gambling dens and cathouses, and then returned to the war undetected.) After the Maceos renovated the Sui Jen in 1942 and renamed it the Balinese Room, it immediately became the swankiest nightspot on the Texas Gulf Coast, replacing the Hollywood Dinner Club. The decor was South Seas, with walls hand-painted to look like tropical beaches and plenty of clamshells and fishnets. Sam Maceo booked the top names in show business—Peggy Lee, Freddy Martin, Jimmy Dorsey, Phil Harris.

The Balinese Room and other nightspots in Galveston had technically become private clubs, which was a way to subvert Texas liquor laws—in the 1940s the law prohibited serving mixed drinks. Membership in most clubs required a modest donation or, often, a dropped name. Sam Maceo made club privilege a key element of his security system. Frank Biaggne, who was sheriff of Galveston County from 1933 to 1957, once explained that he had never raided the Balinese because it was a private club and he was not a member. The Texas Rangers, however, were more worrisome. The casino part of Maceo's operation was located on a T-head, at the end of a two hundred-foot pier. When a raiding party would appear at the bottom of the pier, someone up front pushed a button. On this signal, the bandleader would announce, "And now, the Balinese Room takes great pleasure in presenting . . . in person . . . the Texas Rangers!" at which point his musicians would strike up "The Eyes of Texas" while the gambling paraphernalia folded into the walls like Murphy beds.

One reason the rackets had such a long and successful run in Galveston was Sam Maceo's sense of public relations. Important guests, and sometimes those who were not so important, were entertained royally in his suite at the Hotel Galvez (which he occupied from 1934 to 1938). He donated large sums to every charity on the Island, sent orphans to college, and kept widows from being evicted. He gave generously to the First Methodist Church and made sure that once each year Monsignor Daniel P. O'Connell ("Father Dan"), the rector of St. Mary's Cathedral, got the money to visit his poor old mother in Ireland. When the Mardi Gras committee needed a headliner, Sam delivered Edgar Bergen and Charlie McCarthy. When a French cargo ship loaded with ammonium nitrate exploded at the Port of Texas City, Sam called a few friends and asked them to come to Galveston to help raise money for the victims. Among those who showed up were Frank Sinatra, Jack Benny, Gene Autry, Victor Borge, Jane Russell, George Burns, and Gracie Allen.

Islanders did not merely tolerate the wide-open image of their city; they celebrated it. Paul Burka, the longtime editor of Texas Monthly, was born on the Island (BOI, in local parlance) and remembers that in the mid-1950s kids in junior high looked forward to Tuesday because that was the day that students whose fathers worked for the Maceos would bring football betting cards to school. The Maceos essentially rearranged the Island's physics: the underworld became the overworld. The Maceos were true pillars of the community. Papa Rose was a preferred customer at Moody's City National Bank, able to borrow on his signature alone $100,000 for a shipload of liquor. Nobody worried about law and order, but when people got out of hand they were dealt with by a private enforcement group known as Rose's Night Riders.

One of the darkest days in Galveston history had nothing to do with the weather. On Monday, June 10, 1957, eleven assistant attorneys general and a half dozen Texas Rangers gathered at the Galveston Courthouse. They had come to bust the rackets.

During the previous seven months, undercover agents dispatched to the Island by the state's crusading attorney general, Will Wilson, had infiltrated Galveston's vice dens, gathering evidence. Sam and Rose Maceo were both dead by this time, and the syndicate, which operated from the Turf Athletic Club downtown, was controlled by Maceo nephews and other family members. The rackets had been in steep decline for several years. Many of the top dealers and pit bosses had moved to Las Vegas, and the once-glamorous nightspots had acquired an unpleasant seediness, no longer booking big name entertainment or promising gourmet menus. High rollers had found more attractive places to lose their money.

The task force swept across the Island, armed with axes, sledgehammers, and shotguns, kicking down the doors of the Balinese Room and fifty other gambling houses. Slot machines and dice tables that were not smashed on the spot were loaded onto barges and dumped into the sea. "There was still some gambling for another three or four years," recalled Nick Kralj, who as a young man had been pool manager at the Galvez. "But everything changed after the raid." The raid was, in effect, the coup de grace for the Free State of Galveston, its inglorious demise. Galvestonians have seconded these actions, defeating efforts in recent decades to bring back gambling.

Opposite top left: The famous ventriloquist Edgar Bergen, second from the right, was crowned king of the 1948 Mardi Gras by Mayor Herbert Cartwright (behind dummies Charlie McCarthy and Mortimer Snerd). Top right: In 1950 Sam Maceo, at the right, hosts Frank Sinatra at the Balinese Room. With them are Maceo's business partner Anthony Fertitta and the Academy Award–winning composer Jimmy Van Heusen. Bottom left: Jane Wyatt, at the left, another movie and television star, dines at the Balinese Room. Center: The singer Mel Torme, in the middle, is welcomed to town by Galveston Sheriff Frank Biaggne. Right: The actor Peter Lawford signs an autograph for a fan on the beach in 1948. Left: A couple stops in front of a Hotel Galvez sign advertising its air-conditioned Coffee Shop.

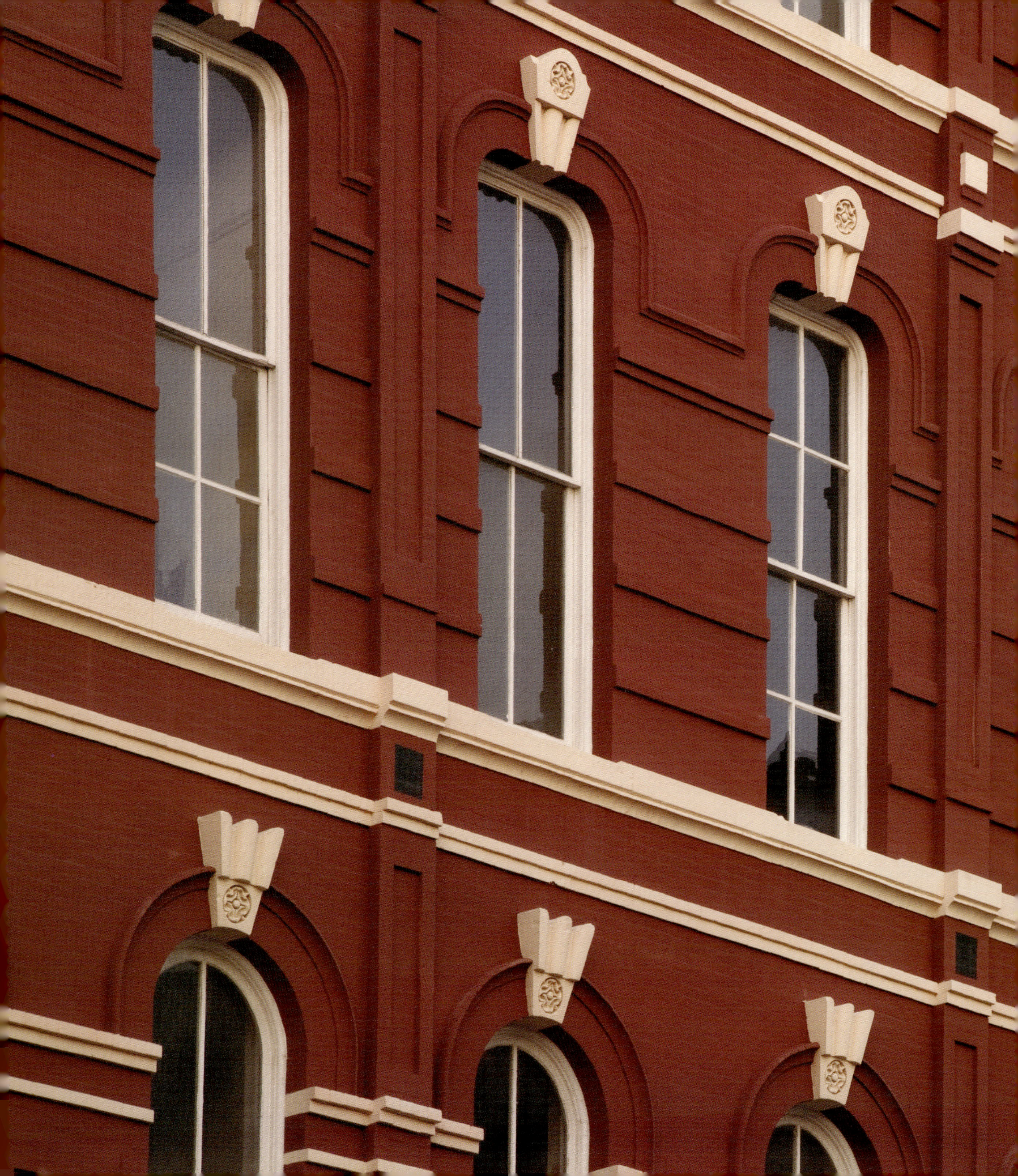

Misfortune and Rebirth

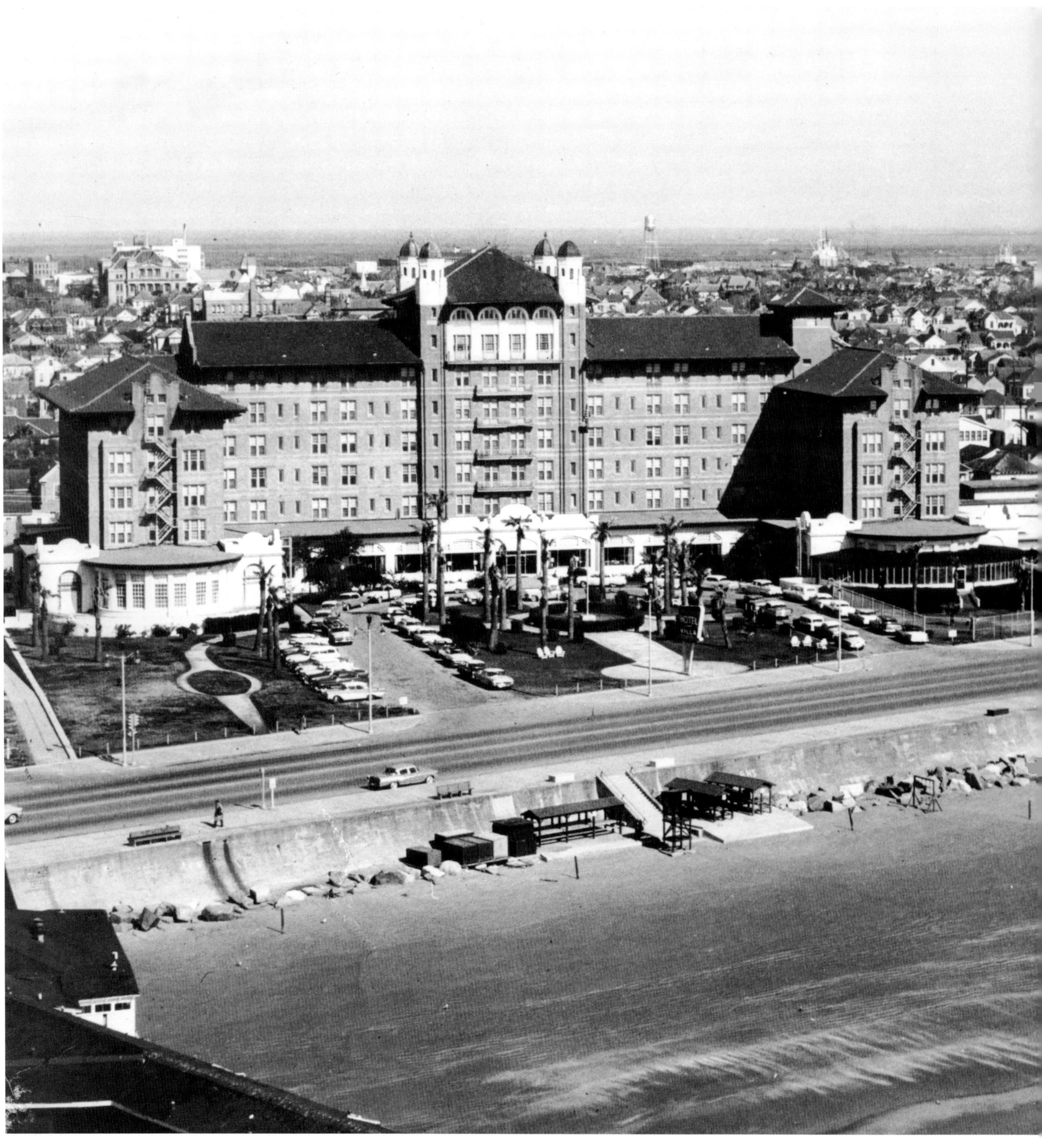

Stormy Years

Galveston's run of bad luck continued for the next thirty years, nearly bankrupting a number of businesses. On two separate occasions, the Galvez itself was forced to shut down. Misfortune seemed to follow misfortune.

Three months after a student-led Splash Day Riot on May 1, 1961, badly damaged the Island's reputation as a family-friendly destination, Hurricane Carla slammed into the state's Gulf Coast. Except for the Great Storm of 1900, Carla was the strongest and deadliest storm ever to strike the United States. Although wind gusts in Galveston were only eighty-eight miles per hour—less than half of the one hundred-seventy-mile-per-hour winds recorded at Port Lavaca—the storm spawned dozens of killer tornadoes, including one F4 tornado that ripped through downtown Galveston, killing at least half a dozen persons.

John Schwartz, who grew up on the Island, remembers that his parents decided to weather the storm at the Hotel Galvez, with their four sons and their dachshund, Teddy. As Schwartz wrote years later as a reporter for the *New York Times*, in a retrospective on hurricanes published just after Hurricane Ike in September 2008, "Seawater sloshed across the lobby.... I woke up with water dripping on my face. We were on the fourth floor . . . but the rains had already soaked through the top floors.... My older brothers and I crouched by a window and watched the waves pluck the heavy benches off of the seawall." John reported that his father, A. R. "Babe" Schwartz, a former state senator, had called the Great Storm of 1900 a "message from God . . . (that) man wasn't meant to live on no damned island."

"Carla took the starch out of the people of Galveston," says Nick Kralj, who later moved to Austin and became a political consultant and lobbyist. "We'd never seen anything like it. Carla was the first time my family had evacuated the Island. My grandfather, John Kralj, who came to Galveston right after the 1900 storm—he was an orphan from Croatia—told us that Carla was far worse than the 1915 storm. That one wiped out his restaurant, Four Seasons, which was at Twenty-first and Mechanic. It was years before Galveston recovered from Carla."

By 1970 W. L. Moody Jr. was looking to sell the Hotel Galvez. One newspaper story reported that a New York investor, Lawrence W. Hurwitz, had offered $2 million, but the deal fell through. A year after that, the hotel was sold for $1 million to Harvey McCarty of Rock Island, Illinois, and Leon Bromberg, a physician who was a Galveston native. McCarty was the hotel's fourth owner and the first one without ties to the Island. He apparently planned to convert the Galvez into an apartment building but changed his mind. In 1976 he put it on the market for $2.5 million. There were no takers.

In a 1960s view taken from the Balinese Room pier, the Galvez Villa—an addition designed to modernize the hotel—can be seen at the right.

MISFORTUNE AND REBIRTH

Opening Spring 1980
The Galvez Marriott
228 Rooms, Restaurant, Lounge
Meeting & Banquet Facilities
For Information call 765-7721

By 1978 both Galveston's economy and the condition of the hotel itself had deteriorated. In November that year the Galvez closed for renovation. When it reopened the next summer, its new owners included Archie Bennett Jr., chair of the Houston Port Commission, and the famed Houston heart surgeon Denton Cooley. Their company, the Mariner Corporation, managed the hotel under a franchise agreement with the Marriott chain. The name changed to the Galvez Marriott.

The new owners instituted major changes, the most important of which was a $10 million restoration project that promised to restore the venerable Gulf Coast landmark to a "well-deserved new dignity," one befitting its addition to the National Register of Historic Places in 1979. The idea was to build "a new hotel in an old shell." Over the years rooms on the upper floors had been renovated a number of times, walls moved about, bathrooms added, windows sealed over, tiles and fixtures mismatched. Now the architects decided to divide the eleven-room penthouse (where Sam Maceo had stayed) into four separate suites and to rebuild the remaining 224 rooms with a standard decor and furnishings based on Marriott specifications. For the first time, the eighth floor was also used for upper-level suites.

The vintage lobby and ballrooms on the first floor stayed as they were, but several major changes were made on the street level. The two-story wing of motel rooms put there during the Moody tenure was demolished, restoring balance and historical integrity to the original building. The main entrance was relocated to the porte cochere on the north side, facing the bay. The south entrance on the Gulf side became an "oasis of activity," with ornately shaped indoor and outdoor pools, a sauna, and a pool house. The new pool proved popular at first, but over time diners began complaining about the pervasive odor of chlorine saturating otherwise fine-dining experiences.

When Hurricane Alicia slammed into the Island in August 1983, the Galvez was forced to close again. Nearly four hundred persons rode out the storm in safety inside the hotel, but the damage was extensive. Nearly all the front windows were blown out, and a fourth-floor wall collapsed when its sheetrock became waterlogged. Most of the roof tiles were ripped away, as were some exterior walls. When the hotel reopened in 1984, rumors of its imminent sale circulated.

In 1988 Cooley and Bennett and their partners were forced into bankruptcy and the Galvez was sold at auction. The winning bid of $7.68 million came from Aetna Life Insurance Company, which had held the mortgage on the hotel since 1980.

Opposite top left: The Galvez closed in November 1978 to begin a $10 million restoration. Opposite top right: Architects and contractors meet outside the hotel to discuss the restoration. Opposite bottom: Interior demolition reached the loggia in January 1980. Left top and bottom: At the June 1980 dedication gala, visitors are announced and then mingle around the pool.

From Skid Row to Historic District

By the early 1970s, many people thought that the Galvez was dead. The historic heart of Galveston was also on its last leg. The Strand had become Skid Row, with winos sleeping in the doorways or abandoned lobbies of one of the greatest collections of historic Victorian buildings in the Southwest. The Santa Fe Railroad had shut down its Galveston operation and announced that the site of the wonderful old Santa Fe Building might become a parking lot. Parking lots were the fate of several other historic buildings. A number had burned down, some the victim of arsonists. Amazingly, more than a thousand structures that had survived the 1900 storm were still standing, but few people seemed interested in saving, much less restoring, them.

Then George Mitchell got reintroduced to his native island. Mitchell had moved to Houston, but his Galveston roots were deep and his appetite for entrepreneurship sharp and ready. He recalls that when he and his wife, Cynthia, would drive through the neglected downtown, she would say: "Someone should really do something about preserving those beautiful buildings. It would be such a shame to see them torn down." When Cynthia became involved with the Galveston Historical Foundation in the late 1970s, George joined in. Over the next three decades, he invested more than $125 million in restoring the Island's historic properties, particularly in The Strand Historic District.

Mitchell was one of three sons of a Greek immigrant named Savvas Paraskevopoulos, who came to the United States in 1901, worked on a railroad crew (where he adopted his Irish paymaster's name, Mike Mitchell), and settled in Galveston. Like most enterprising young people who find themselves native to an island, George, born in 1919 to Savvas and Katina Eleftheriou, made it his passion to explore the place from end to end. He collected seashells on West Beach and sold them to a dealer on Seawall Boulevard. He picked up and resold pop bottles on the beach beneath Murdoch's Pier. At age twelve he spent his summer riding his bike all over the Island, seeing how many varieties of oleander he could identify. "I counted twenty-eight varieties," he remembers. "It's probably thirty-five or forty by now."

In 1990 the Port of Galveston dedicated a cruise ship terminal for ships operating in the Caribbean. Today the terminal is a home port for Carnival Cruise Lines and Royal Caribbean International.

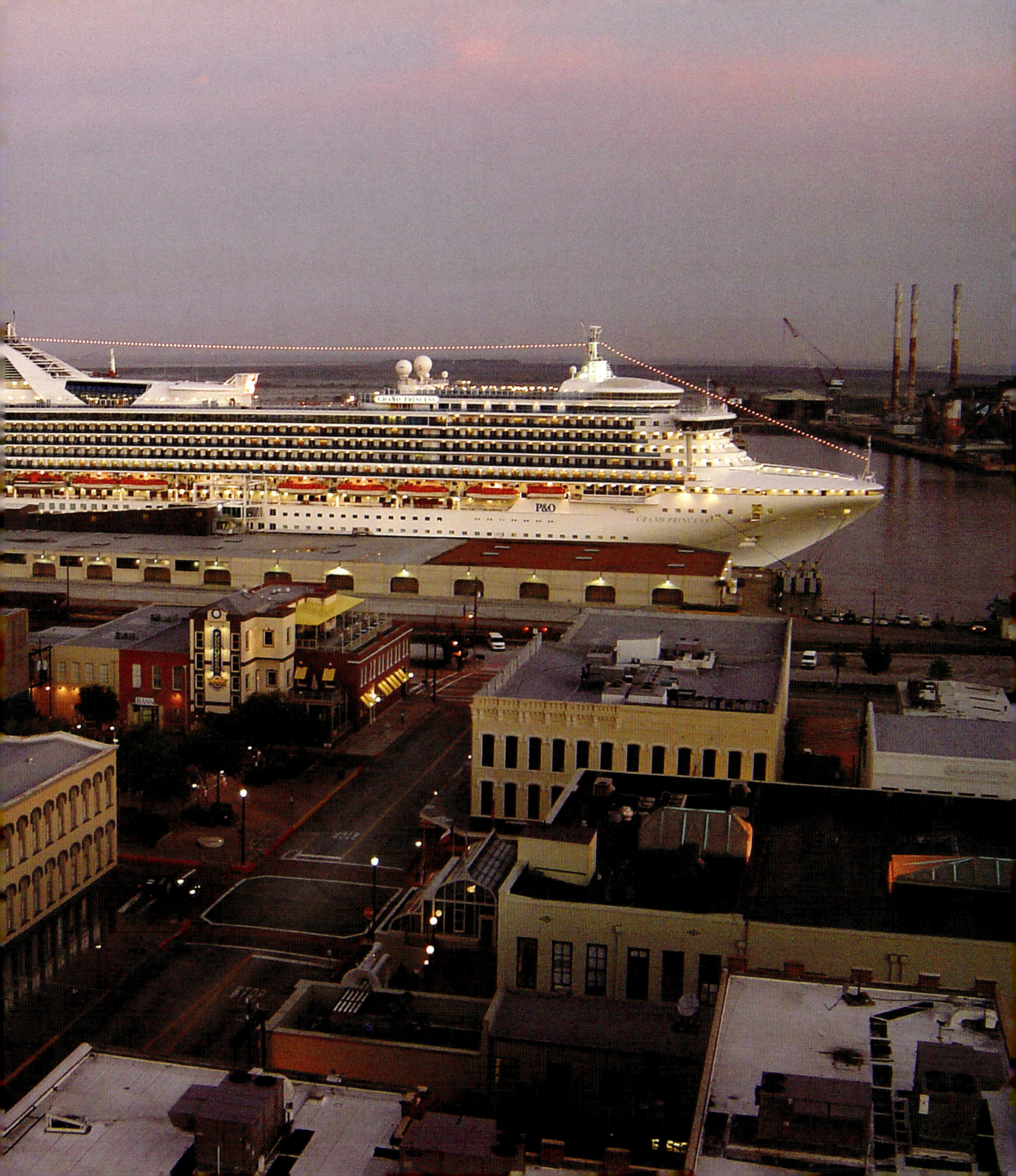
P&O

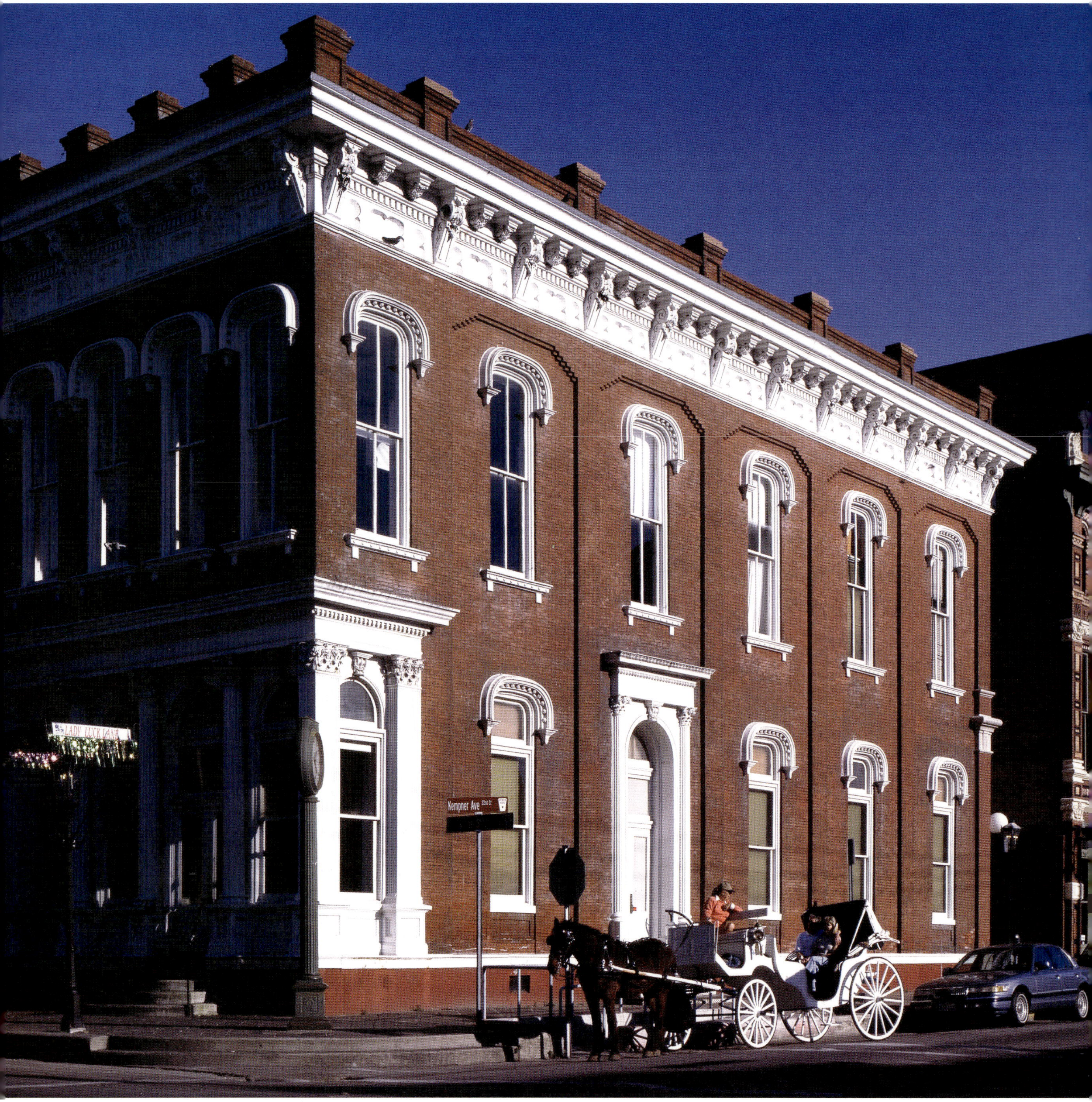
LADY LUCK LANE
Kempner Ave
22nd St

Left: Victorian buildings in The Strand, a National Historic Landmark District, house restaurants, galleries, shops, and public spaces such as the Galveston Arts Center at the far left. Above: Cynthia and George Mitchell, seen in front of the Blum Building (later The Tremont House) reinvigorated preservation efforts in the district.

George's mother wanted him to be a doctor. The summer before he was to enroll at Rice as a premed major, Mitchell joined his brother Johnny in the oil fields of Louisiana and got oil fever. He decided to go to Texas A&M instead and study petroleum engineering. After serving in the Army Corps of Engineers in World War II, he hooked up with a group of wildcatters, including his brother Johnny and Big Sam Maceo, and began to drill in Wise County. In 1953, acting on a tip from a Chicago bookie, their company discovered one of the industry's largest gas strikes ever, the Boonville gas field northwest of Fort Worth. Once he had established himself in the petroleum business, Mitchell turned his talents to building and renovating urban areas. Among other projects, he developed The Woodlands in Houston in 1974 and Pirates Cove, a resort community on the west end of Galveston Island, along with other west-end properties.

MISFORTUNE AND REBIRTH · 99

By the early 1970s Galvestonians had started a grassroots preservation effort, rescuing Ashton Villa (1859) and the Bishop's Palace (1893), among other landmarks. On The Strand, Sally and Jack Wallace had already saved a section of the Hendley Building (1859), and the Junior League had adopted the Trueheart-Adriance Building (1882) and the adjacent First National Bank Building (1878), now the Galveston Arts Center. Then the Moody Foundation, working with the Arts Council and Kempner interests, provided a major grant to establish The Strand Revolving Fund. The Galveston Historical Foundation brought in Peter H. Brink as its executive director, including oversight of the revolving fund. Restructured, the foundation was blessed with a series of outstanding volunteer leaders, including Evangeline Whorton and the public relations whiz Dancie Ware.

Revitalization of The Strand took on huge new potential in 1976 when George and Cynthia Mitchell bought the deteriorated Thomas Jefferson League Building (1871) from the revolving fund. It was converted into the Wentletrap Restaurant, named in a family contest by the Mitchells' daughter Sheridan Mitchell Lorenz, who had just read about a seashell known as Mitchell's Wentletrap. Sheridan and her nine brothers and sisters grew up in Houston but spent their summers on the Island, in a neighborhood called Fish Village, in a house built by the famed Texas architect O'Neil Ford.

At the urging of Dancie Ware, the Mitchells took on ever-larger projects. These included the conversion in 1985 of the Leon and H. Blum Building (1879), which was literally on the verge of collapse after Hurricane Alicia. Working with the architect Boone Powell of Ford, Powell and Carson, the Mitchells turned the former wholesale dry-goods emporium into The Tremont House, a 119-room luxury hotel with fifteen suites spread over an entire block in The Strand Historic District; Cynthia Mitchell and Dancie Ware played key roles in the hotel's interior design. George Mitchell held a grand party to celebrate the return of Galveston's historic Tremont House, whose two predecessors on the Island (dating to 1839 and 1872) had fallen to fire and ruin. He also led a movement to bring back Mardi Gras as a show of faith in the Island's rebirth and supported restoration of the barque *Elissa* (1877), now one of Galveston's leading tourist attractions as well as an operating sailing vessel with hundreds of volunteers. And for good measure Mitchell helped finance the return of the rail trolley, which runs from The Strand to the beach. In the aftermath of Hurricane Ike in 2008, Mitchell Historic Properties again stepped in, leading a massive, $24 million cleanup and renovation of some two dozen damaged historic buildings.

Salvaged after Hurricane Alicia, the former Blum Building (1879) was adapted for hotel use by the Mitchells. Their elegant Tremont House, nestled in the heart of Galveston's Strand Historic District, opened in 1985 and features a four-story atrium lobby with birdcage elevators, ironwork balconies, and tropical palm trees.

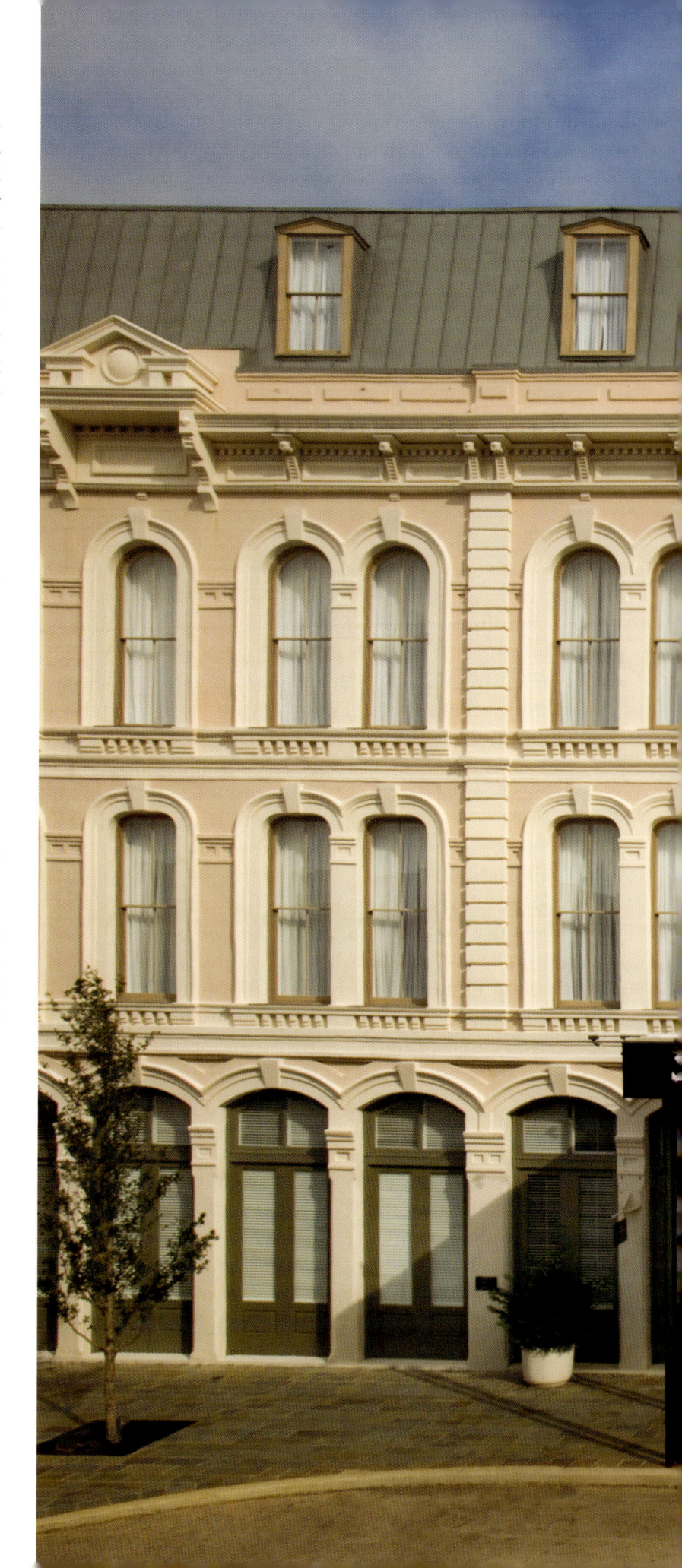

THE TREMONT HOUSE

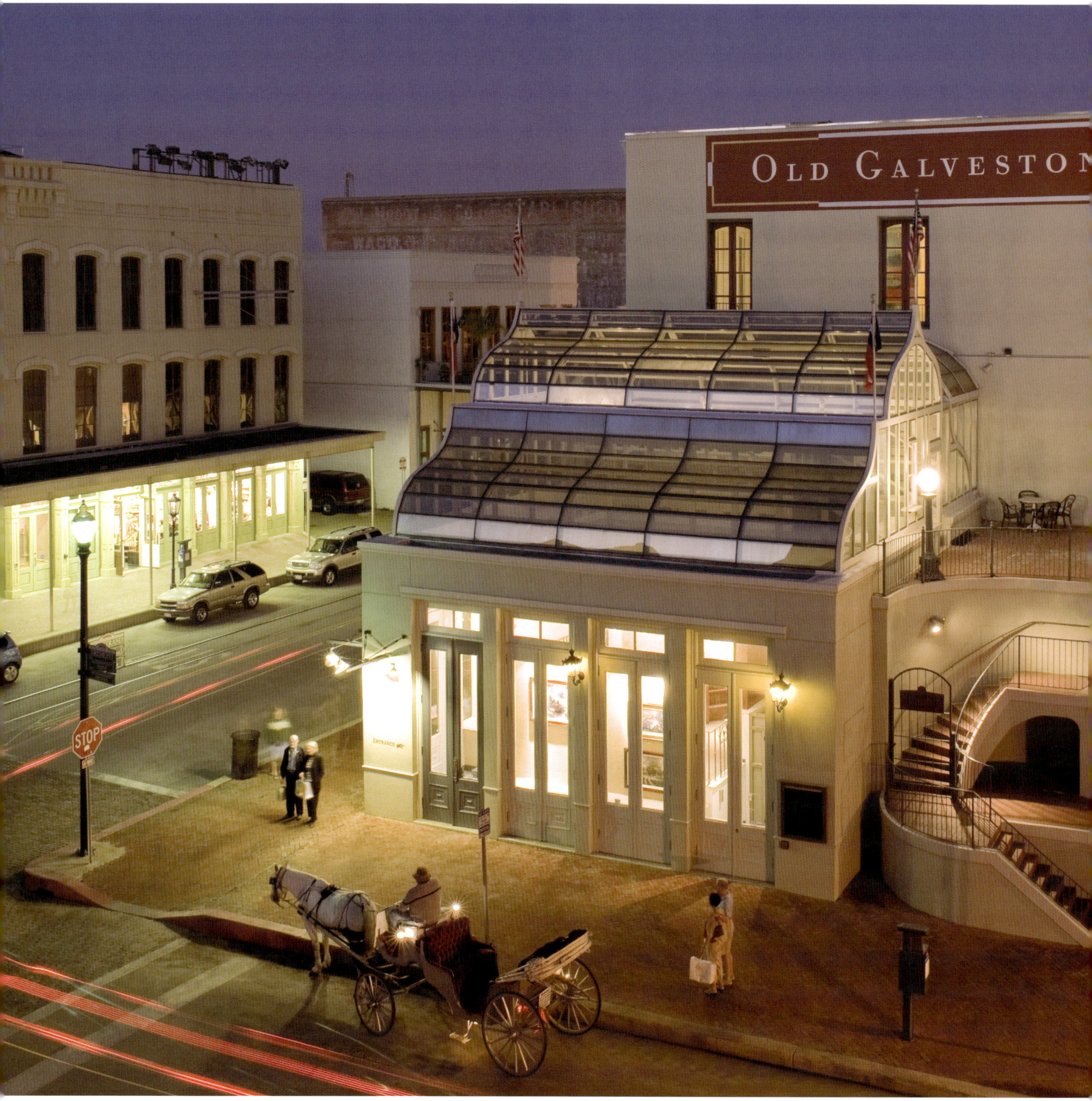
OLD GALVESTON
STOP

One of George Mitchell's most ambitious projects started with the purchase of twenty-two acres of old Fort Crockett along the seawall, including the fort's World War II gun emplacements with elevated bunkers and seven-foot-wide concrete walls. On top of the bunkers Mitchell built the fifteen-story San Luis Hotel, which by the time it opened in June 1984 had cost $38 million. To replenish the badly eroded beach in front of the new hotel, he ordered truckloads of white sand—fifteen thousand cubic feet of it—to replace what had washed away; over time, the new sand also washed away, and Mitchell periodically had it replaced until the city began to issue bonds in 1990 covering beach renourishment. (He later sold this hotel to Tilman Fertitta, a relative of the Maceos.)

In 2009, in recognition of his role in the renaissance of Galveston's Strand and other historic buildings, George Mitchell was awarded the Spirit of Galveston Award by the Galveston Chamber of Commerce. In presenting the award at the Hotel Galvez, Maureen Patton, the chamber's treasurer, declared: "We are blessed in countless ways as individuals, nonprofit organizations, and businesses to embrace George Mitchell, he of the unwavering commitment to our Island, his unsinkable optimism, and yes, his indomitable spirit that has shaped his life and ours."

Left: Heralded by a steel and concrete cornet designed by the Texas artist David Adickes, the Old Galveston Square buildings were adapted by the Mitchells for retail use. Above: The Galveston Historical Foundation restored the 1877 Tall Ship *Elissa* as a fully functional vessel that periodically sails in the Gulf of Mexico.

"Good Enough for Everybody and Not Too Good for Anybody"

In the early 1990s, when rumors were circulating that a group of investors from Vietnam was negotiating to buy the Galvez, Cynthia Mitchell said to her husband, "If you really care about Galveston, you'll buy the Galvez." As Mitchell later recalled: "I knew she was right. I paid Aetna $3 million, and then spent another $20 million fixing it up. I decided that the Galvez was worth my best effort."

Even before the deal was done, the Mitchells began studying old photographs of how the hotel looked in 1911. "It was open and airy, with dark wood tables and bentwood chairs in the dining room," Sheridan Mitchell Lorenz relates. "The great halls and reception rooms were filled with white wicker, lots of light, those great arches, and big open windows. In one of the previous renovations, the windows were replaced with plate glass, the top arched part of the windows hidden behind plaster, and the entire window covered with heavy drapes. Our first goal was to get rid of the drapes and then we totally replaced the windows."

Under Cynthia Mitchell's direction, the architects, Boone Powell of Ford, Powell and Carson in San Antonio and Michael Gaertner of Michael Gaertner and Associates in Galveston, wisely decided to remove the indoor swimming pool and construct a new tropical water oasis, with a swim-up bar and the Seaside Grille, on the lawn beneath the Veranda. The task of restoring the hotel's circular grand entrance to its rightful place facing the Gulf was undertaken by SLA Studio Land.

Above: Palm trees line the entrance to the Hotel Galvez, which was restored by George and Cynthia Mitchell after their 1993 purchase of the landmark. Right: More palms can be found at the pool, which features a swim-up bar as well as a hot tub and cabanas.

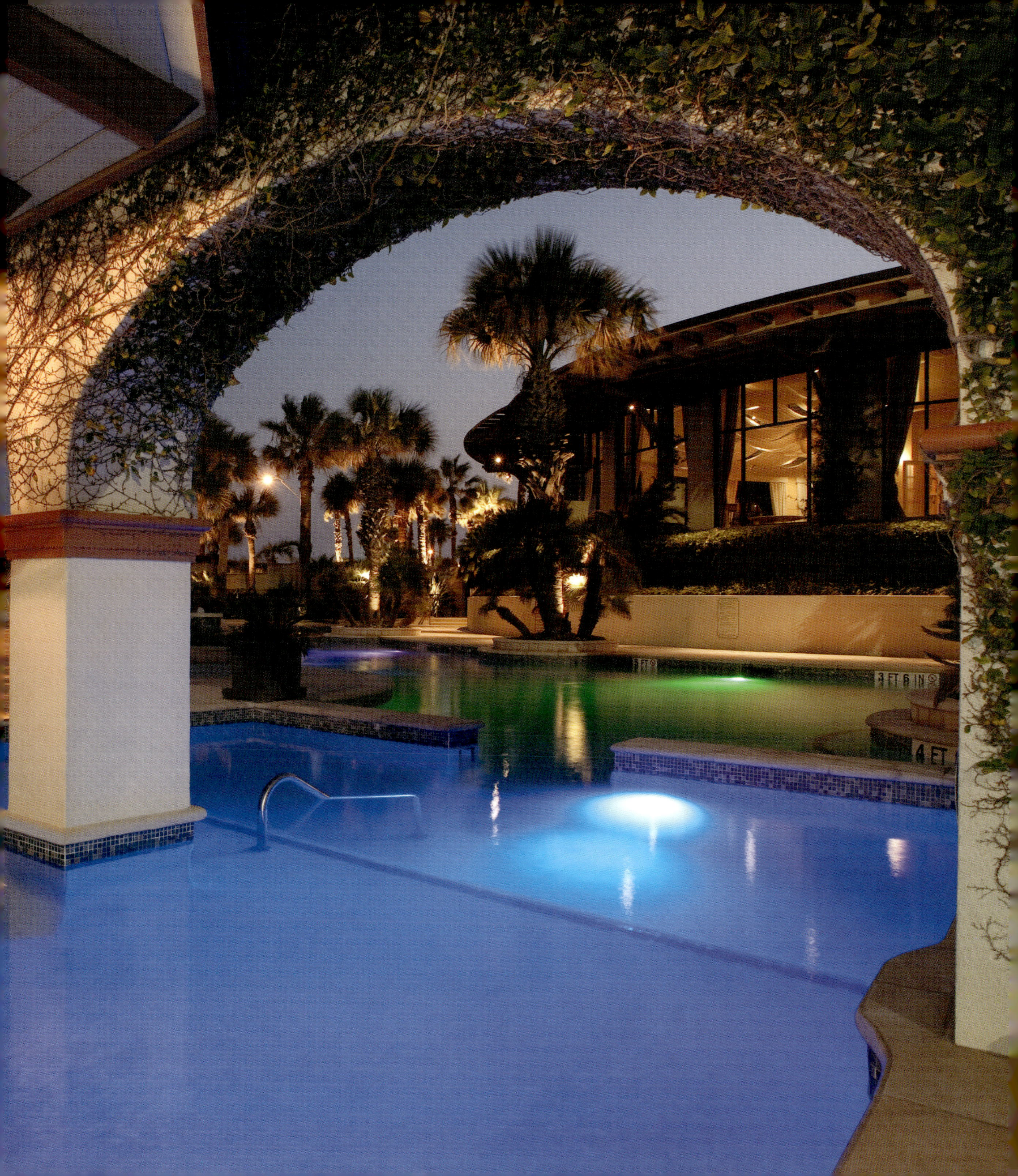
3 FT 6 IN

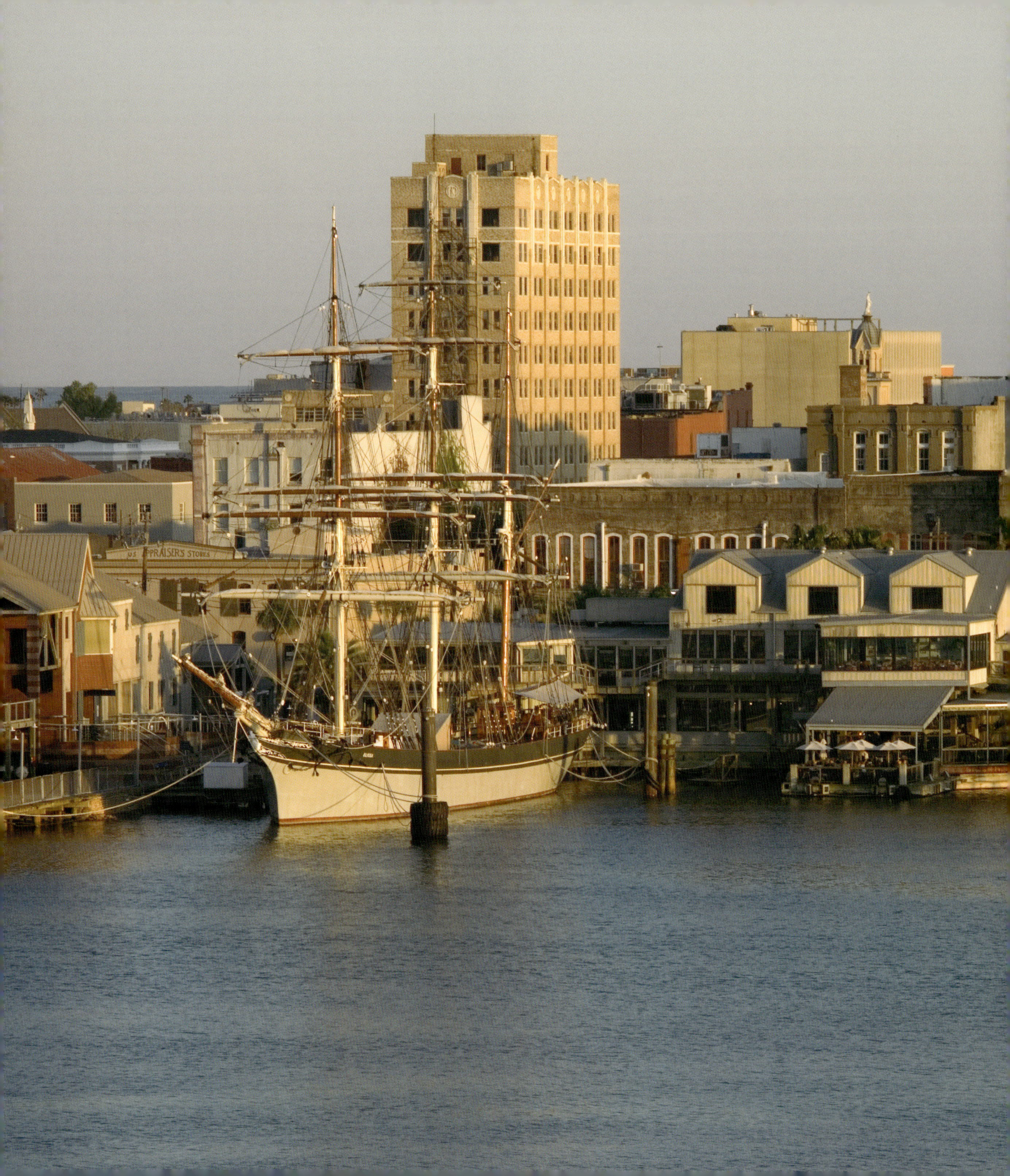
STORES

Interior renovations were carried out to recreate the 1911 feel of the hotel with modern materials. Historical research helped replicate original colors, finishes, and details. The lobby and foyer were expanded to recapture their original size and grandeur. With its new-old Lobby Bar picking up the tones of the ceiling's mahogany beams, the lobby features new furniture and custom-designed carpeting. In the two parlors off the loggias, used today for small meetings, ornate plaster crown moldings were restored.

Today Mitchell Historic Properties owns three hotels on the Island—the Hotel Galvez and Spa, The Tremont House, and the Harbor House Hotel and Marina (1993)—as well as twenty buildings in The Strand National Historic Landmark District. The Hotel Galvez and Spa, however, remains special. Surveying the sweep and the grandeur of this building as it marks its centennial, one is overwhelmed with the sensation of discovering a vintage postcard of a glorious and perhaps forbidden adventure, stuck away in a family attic. The Galvez is a reminder of another age, the work of a generation that understood some concepts that subsequent generations nearly lost—architectural refinement, the welcome appeal of Southern hospitality, and resilience in the face of repeated misfortune.

Left: In the late 1800s, The Strand was the banking, retail, and shipping hub of the region and was known throughout the country as the Wall Street of the Southwest. Today the Mitchell family owns twenty beautifully restored historic buildings in The Strand National Historic Landmark District. Nearby Galveston Harbor and the Pier 21 area form one boundary of Galveston's historic downtown. Above: The Hotel Galvez nameplate over the north porte cochere has welcomed a century of visitors.

Soup's On!

The Hotel Galvez is widely known for its long-standing Sunday brunch, which features an impressive array of seafood, fruit and cheese trays, assorted breads, a carving station, an omelet station, and tempting dessert selections. The chef's award-winning gumbo is offered daily at Bernardo's restaurant and is frequently featured on the brunch menu.

Top and above: A carved ice sculpture and a platter of crab claws lend festive notes to the Sunday brunch presentation. Right: Executive Chef Jerry Helminski presides over the weekly feast at Bernardo's.

108 · MISFORTUNE AND REBIRTH

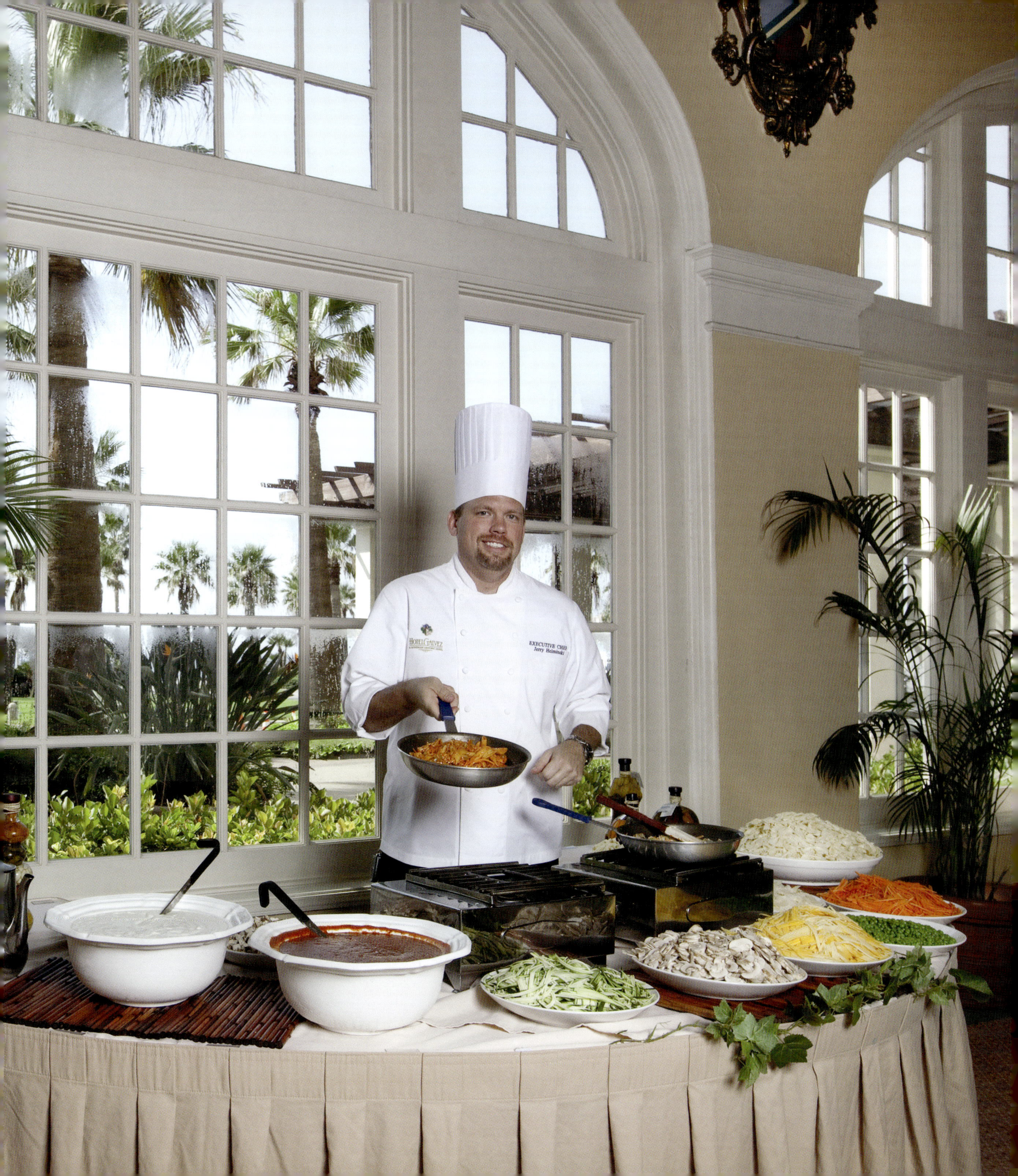

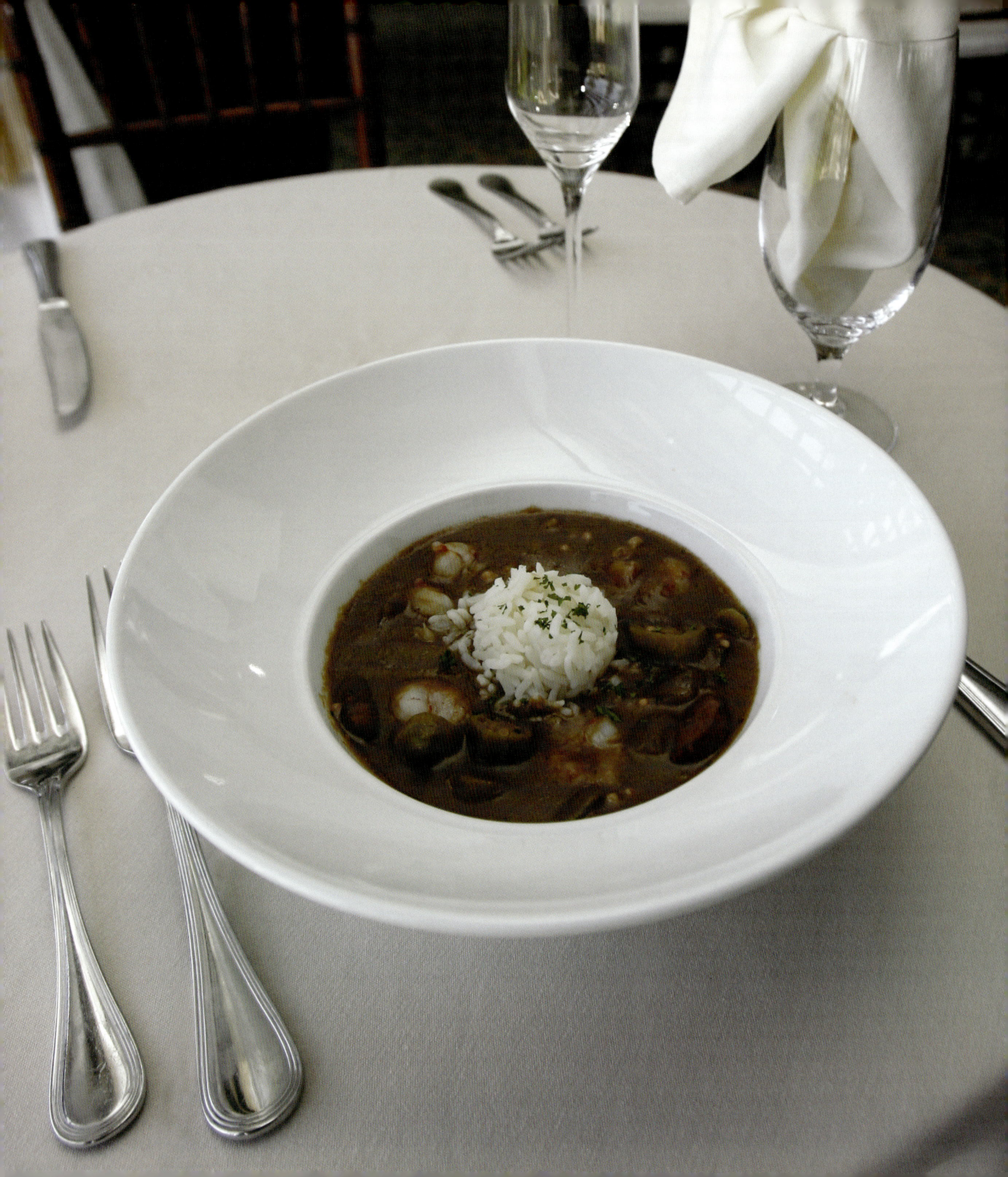

Bernardo's Gumbo

1 cup salad oil
1 cup all-purpose flour
2 yellow onions, diced ½"
3 green bell peppers, diced ½"
4 celery stalks, diced ½"
6 garlic cloves, peeled and minced
2 quarts chicken stock
2 quarts seafood stock
2 pounds rock shrimp, uncooked
2 pounds Andouille sausage, sliced
1 pound okra (fresh or frozen), sliced
2 teaspoons Cajun seasoning
2 teaspoons paprika
1 teaspoon cayenne pepper
1 teaspoon dried thyme
1 teaspoon dried oregano
1 teaspoon onion powder
1 teaspoon garlic powder
1 teaspoon Creole seasoning
½ teaspoon Old Bay seasoning
1 tablespoon red Tabasco sauce
1 tablespoon green Tabasco sauce

1. In a heavy-bottom stock pot, combine the oil and flour and heat at medium-low, stirring occasionally, until the roux is dark brown (up to 45 minutes). Be careful not to burn the flour.

2. While the roux is browning, bake the Andouille sausage in a 350-degree oven for 5 minutes. Drain any excess grease, and set aside the sausage.

3. Once the roux is the desired color, add the sausage, onion, green pepper, and celery. Stir constantly to incorporate the sausage, roux, and vegetables.

4. Mix together all the dry seasonings and the garlic. Add to the roux mixture and cook for 2 minutes, until the seasoning is fragrant.

5. Slowly add the chicken and seafood stock, stirring constantly. Bring the liquid to a boil and then reduce it to a low simmer. Cook for approximately 1 hour.

6. Add the shrimp and the okra, cooking an additional 10 minutes or until the shrimp are cooked.

7. Adjust to taste with red and green Tabasco sauce.

8. Serve hot over steamed rice.

Serves 12.

Opposite: The hotel's delectable gumbo conjures up the flavors of Creole cuisine. Top and above: The china and serving dishes featured in the hotel's original Marine Dining Room included the Bernardo de Gálvez coat of arms. Pink oleanders curl around a dinner plate and a soup tureen from 1911.

MISFORTUNE AND REBIRTH · 111

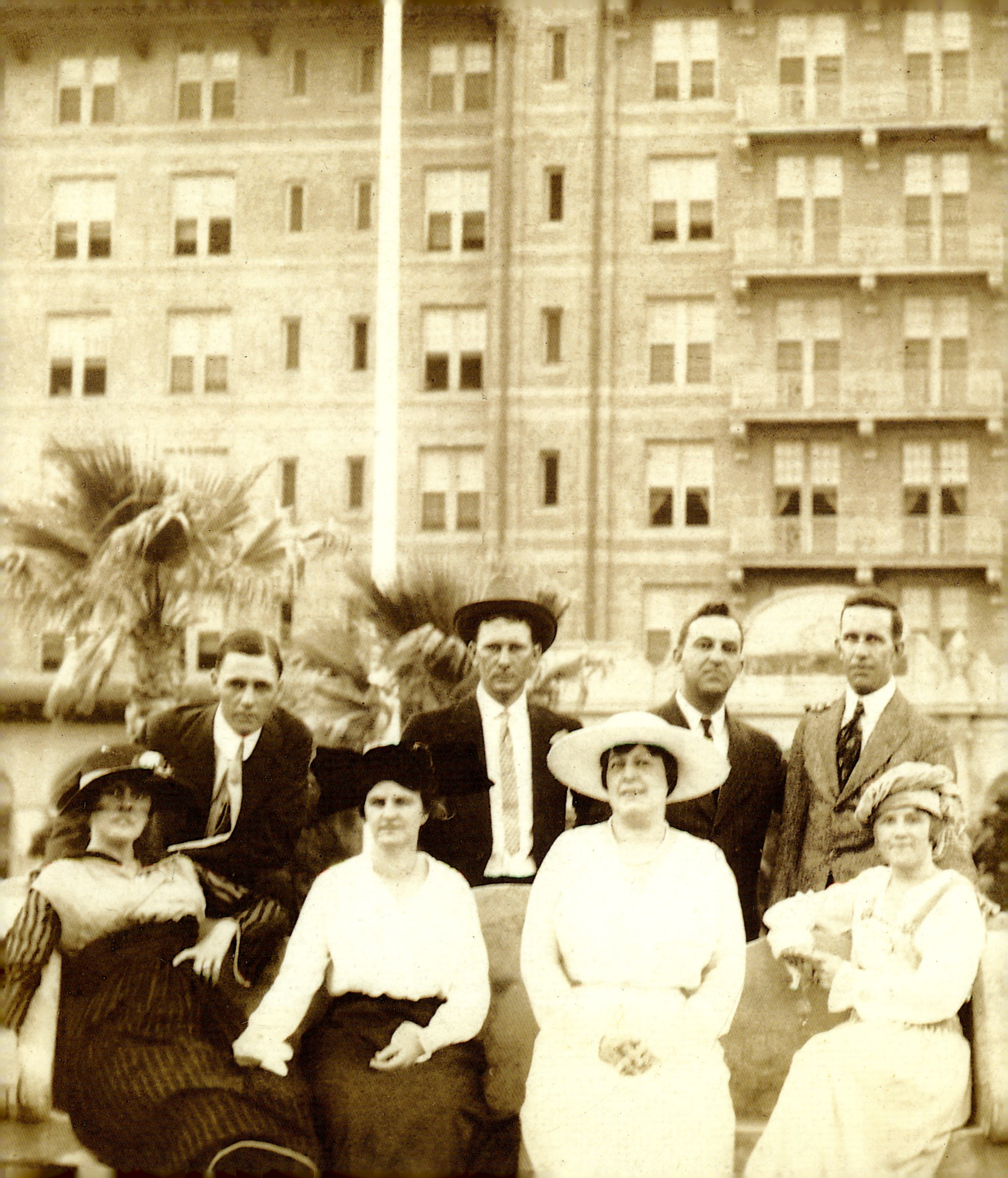

Ghosts and Other Guests

Big Shots

It was always big news when a national celebrity visited the Galvez, bigger still when the celebrity was the president of the United States. The social event of 1937 was the arrival of Franklin D. Roosevelt. Regardless of politics or party affiliation, nearly everyone on the Island raced to make the president's trip a memorable one. Ike Kempner turned the Galvez into a temporary White House and made it the media capital of the United States. W. L Moody Jr. invited F.D.R., who arrived on his presidential yacht, the U.S.S. *Potomac*, to join him on a fishing trip. George Sealy, who had identified hundreds of varieties of oleander, named one of the plants after the president.

No doubt Sam Maceo would have invited F.D.R. to one of his clubs, except that Sam was in New York, facing federal narcotics charges. The feds had arrested him at his penthouse suite in the Galvez. It turned out that the drugs had been planted in Sam's car by a local prostitute, in an attempt to frame him. Sam was eventually acquitted, with the aid of the Galveston lawyer Louis Dibrell and some high-priced New York legal talent.

The Island went similarly nuts in December 1949, when General (and future president) Dwight D. Eisenhower came to town. Ike spoke at the Pleasure Pier's Marine Room to a crowd of two thousand, after which he was swept off to a reception at the Hotel Galvez. He was booked into the Presidential Suite, where he gave interviews but apparently did not spend the night. According to newspaper accounts, the oilman Sid Richardson met Ike at the hotel late that same day and took him off to Rockport for some quail hunting.

In June 1955 Vice President Richard Nixon stayed at the Galvez during a speaking engagement to members of the Texas Press Association. In September 1959, Senator Lyndon Baines Johnson and his staff occupied suite 220. On a less auspicious occasion, but still part of the Galvez lore, Jimmy Webb, composer of the song "Galveston," arrived at the Galvez in April 1969, in preparation for acting as grand marshal for the Island's Shrimp Festival.

Other noted celebrities to have signed the Galvez guest register include Douglas "Wrong Way" Corrigan, Sammy Davis Jr., Jimmy Dorsey, Duke Ellington, Phil Harris and Alice Faye, Howard Hughes, Peggy Lee, Jerry Lewis, General Douglas MacArthur, Dean Martin, Freddy Martin, Frank Sinatra, and Jimmy Stewart.

Right: Three presidents—Franklin D. Roosevelt, Dwight D. Eisenhower, and Lyndon B. Johnson—have figured in the hotel's history. Opposite top: Sam Maceo and children Sedgie, Jay-R, and Eddie, beside Mayor J. Curtis Trahan and Marjorie Reynolds, greet Phil Harris, Alice Faye, and Jack Benny. Center: Also welcomed at the hotel were General Douglas MacArthur; Dean Martin, Sammy Davis Jr., and Frank Sinatra; and Douglas "Wrong Way" Corrigan. Bottom: Duke Ellington, Howard Hughes, and Jimmy Webb are also among the hotel's notable guests.

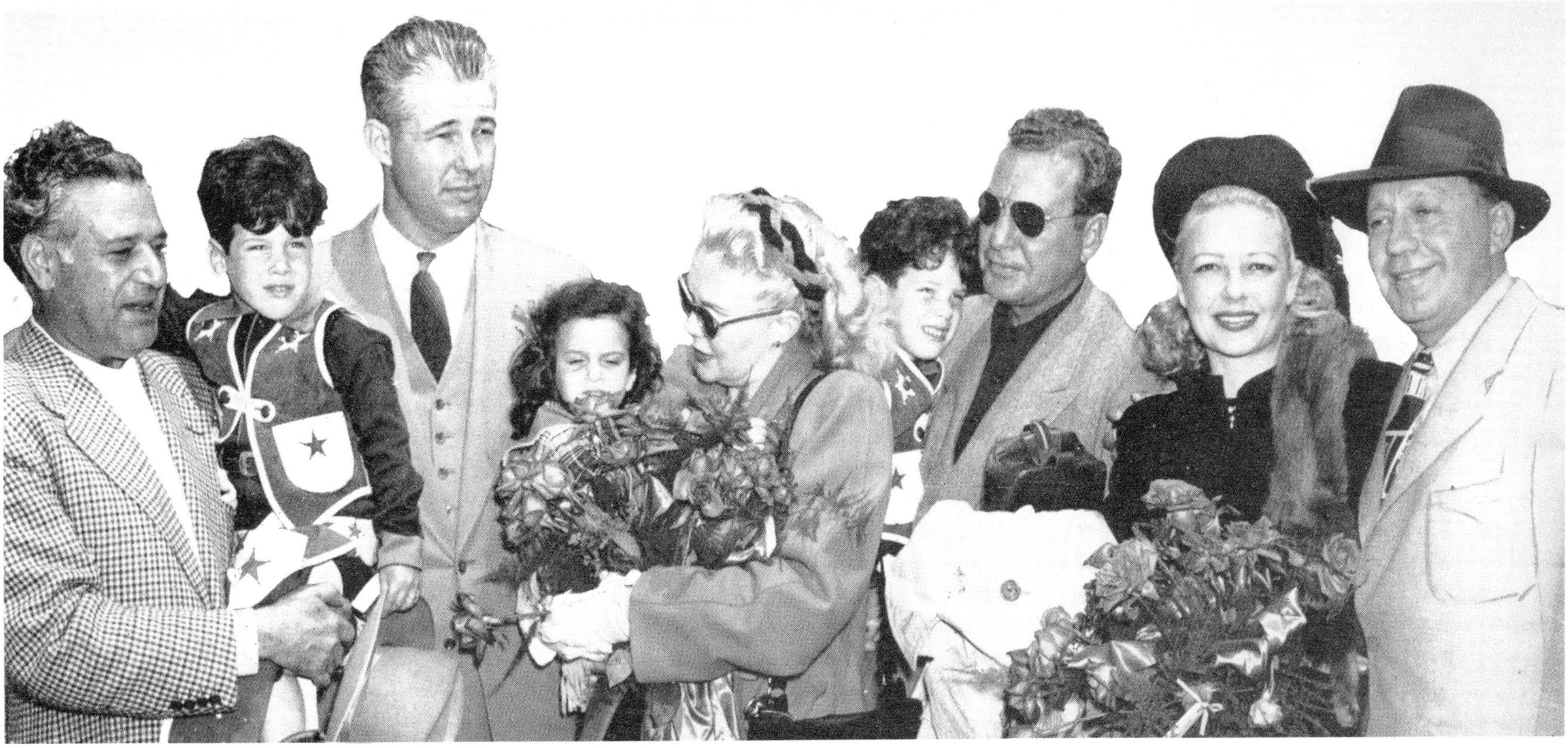

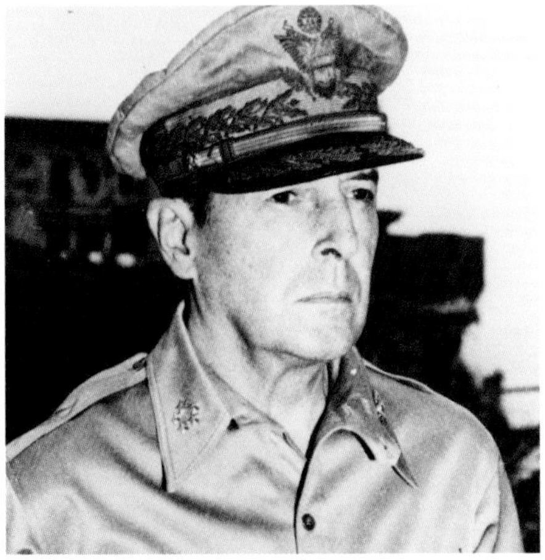

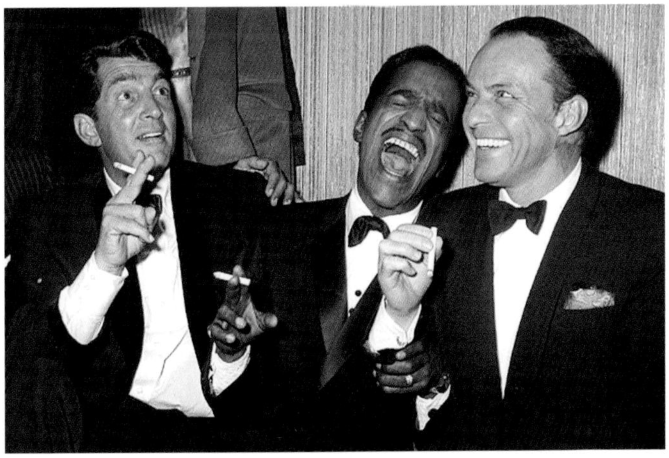

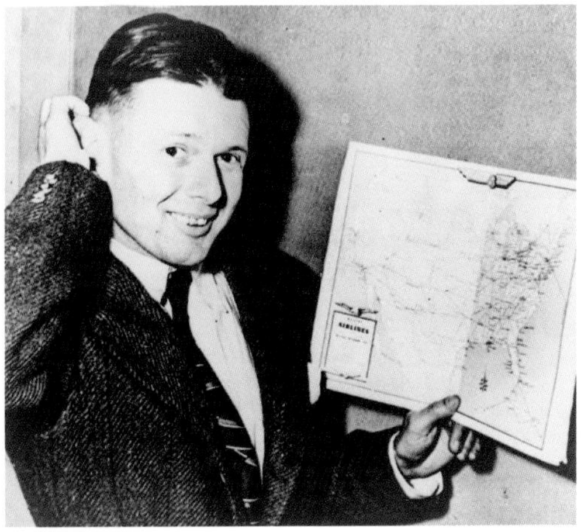

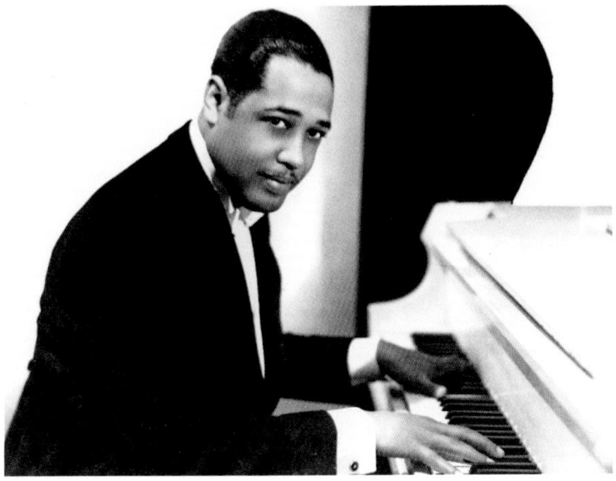

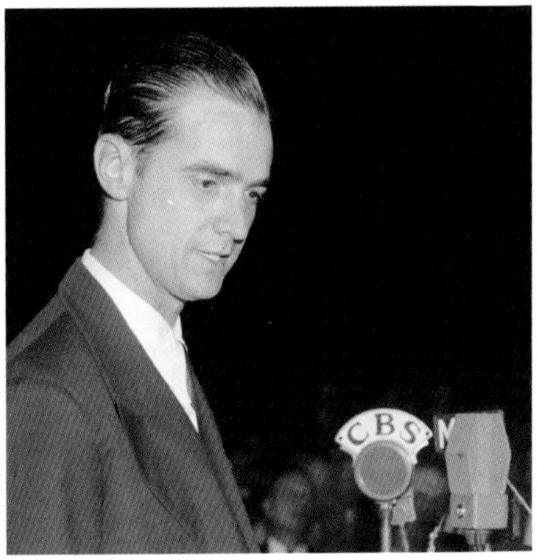
CBS

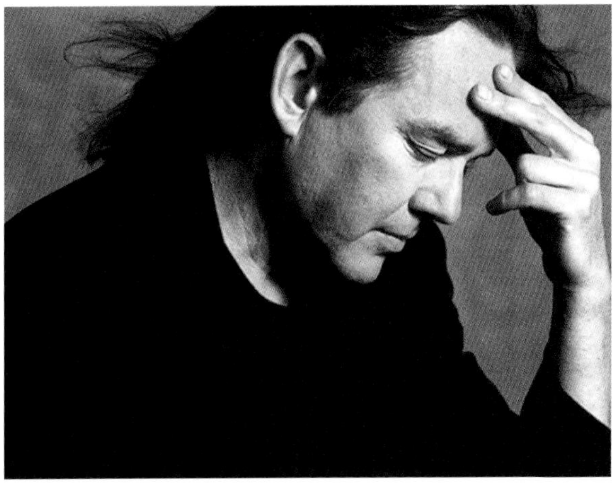

The Ghost Bride of Room 501

Every great hotel must have its ghost, and the Hotel Galvez has one who has been around at least a half century. According to Jan Johnson (a fifth-generation Galvestonian and the author of *Walking Historic Galveston*), the Galvez ghost could be a bride-to-be named Audra. Legend has it that she was about twenty-five years old and stayed in Room 501. Then tragedy befell her.

In the mid-1950s, Audra was engaged to a mariner who sailed in and out of the Port of Galveston. Whenever his ship was due in port, she would leave Room 501, take an elevator to the eighth floor, and climb the narrow ladder that opened into one of the four metal-ribbed hexagonal turrets that sit at each corner of the main red-tiled roof. Sheltered from the weather, she would wait inside the turret and watch through an opening for her lover's ship.

Then there was a mighty storm and for days no word of his ship. Finally Audra heard that the ship had gone down and that all hands were lost. She refused to abandon hope, however, and continued to climb to the roof each day, praying for some sign. But no ship was ever sighted. In despair, according to legend, she hanged herself in the west turret.

But that was only half of the tragedy. A few days after her death, her mariner appeared at the hotel, very much alive and looking forward to a marriage that was never to be.

Nearly everyone on the hotel staff has heard the story and some believe that it is true. "Her spirit is locked inside the hotel—she never crossed over," suggested the senior concierge, Jackie Hasan, who was born on the Island and is the fourth generation of her family to work at the Galvez. Hasan has felt the presence not only of the Ghost Bride but also of other spirits who dwell at the hotel. "My father was a mortician," she explained, "and I think my familiarity with death makes the spirits feel comfortable with me and me with them."

Hasan conducts ghost tours and encourages guests to keep an eye out for orbs of light and other paranormal features. A popular part of the tour is a walk down the west loggia, where the large oil painting of Bernardo de Gálvez, with its hauntingly riveting eyes, dominates the wall outside the Music Hall. Nearby, on the wall next to the ladies' restroom, a photograph taken in 1911 shows a ghostly figure of a woman seated alone at the end of the hallway, together with some orbs of light on one of the ceiling beams.

Letters arrive regularly at Hasan's desk in the hotel lobby from guests who report spooky but usually thrilling experiences during their stay. Many enclose photographs that, they claim, reveal orbs—faint globes of light on walls or beams. Nonbelievers see only an occasional smear on the negative—and often nothing at all.

For a place that is supposedly haunted, Room 501 is one of the most requested rooms at the Galvez. A steady stream of believers, skeptics, reporters, and psychic mediums spend time there, hoping to meet the Ghost Bride themselves. In October 2009 a paranormal from Baytown, Freda Little, spent a night in 501, at which time a friend took a cellphone photograph of the bed. "We could not believe our eyes when the picture appeared, showing a fully formed ghost image of a man and a woman lying in bed!" Hasan related.

Reports such as this one not withstanding, no one has added much to the legend—suggesting that like ghosts the world over, the ghosts at the Hotel Galvez are only as real as you want them to be.

Postcard 1 (front):

Hotel Galvez, $1,000,000 Beach Hotel, overlooking The Great Galveston Sea Wall and Gulf of Mexico, Galveston, Texas.

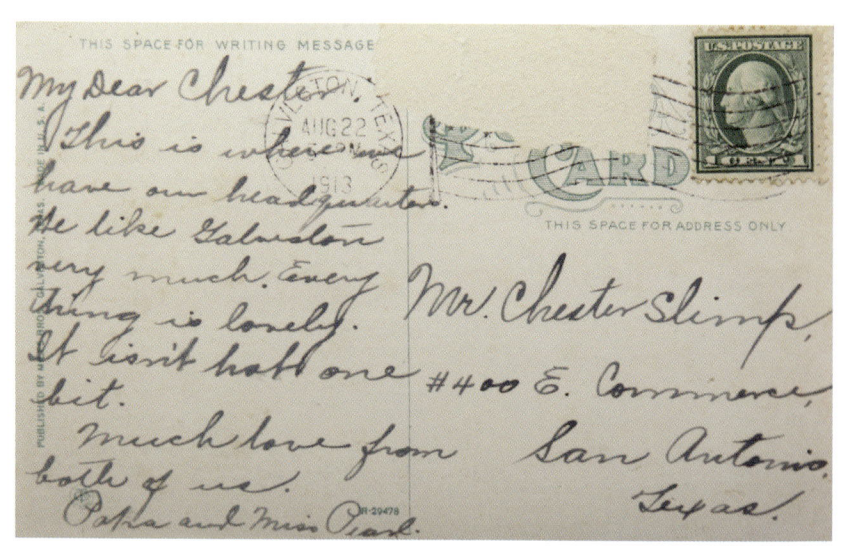

Postcard 2 (back):

My Dear Chester,
This is where we have our headquarters. We like Galveston very much. Everything is lovely. It isn't hot one bit.
Much love from both of us.
Papa and Miss Pearl

Mr. Chester Slimp,
#400 E. Commerce,
San Antonio,
Texas.

Postmark: Galveston, Tex. AUG 22 1913

Postcard 3 (back):

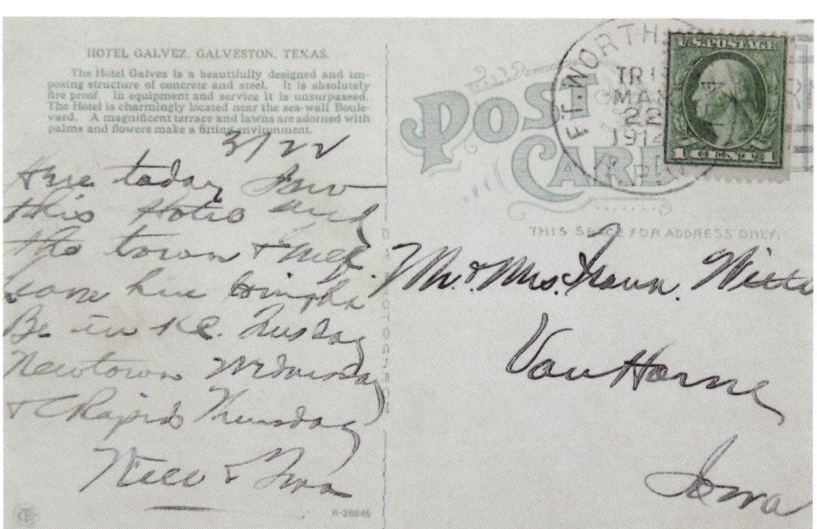

HOTEL GALVEZ, GALVESTON, TEXAS.
The Hotel Galvez is a beautifully designed and imposing structure of concrete and steel. It is absolutely fire proof. In equipment and service it is unsurpassed. The Hotel is charmingly located near the sea-wall Boulevard. A magnificent terrace and lawns are adorned with palms and flowers make a fitting environment.

Are today. Saw this Hotel and the town & met some here tonight. Be in K.C. Sunday, Newtown Monday & Rapids Tuesday.
Nell & Ora

Mr. & Mrs. Frank Witte
Van Horne
Iowa

Postmark: Ft. Worth MAR 22 1912

Postcard 4 (front):

7321. Hotel Galvez, Galveston, Tex.

Postcard 5 (front):

Hotel Galvez, overlooking the Great Seawall and the Gulf of Mexico, Galveston Texas 109

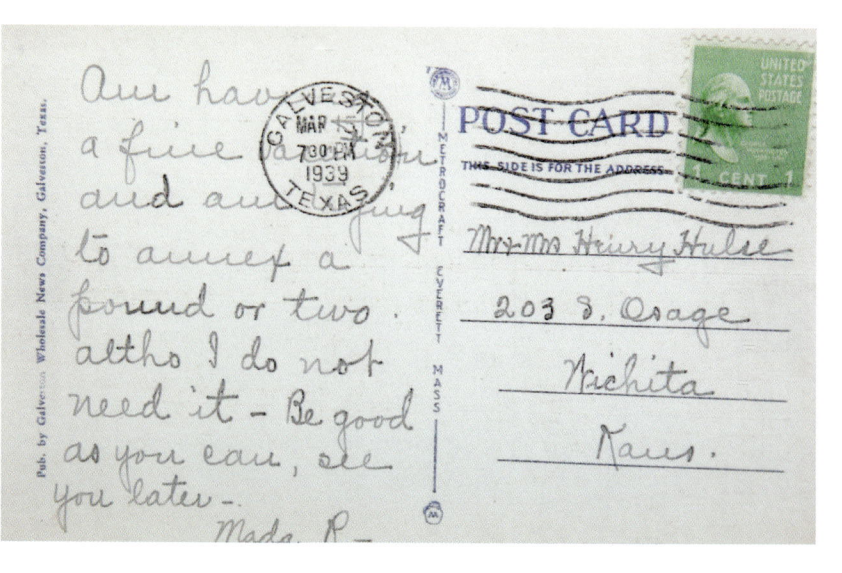

Postcard 6 (back):

Am having a fine vacation, and am trying to annex a pound or two, altho I do not need it — Be good as you can, see you later —
Mada R—

Mr. & Mrs. Henry Hulse
203 S. Osage
Wichita
Kans.

Postmark: Galveston, Texas MAR 2 1939

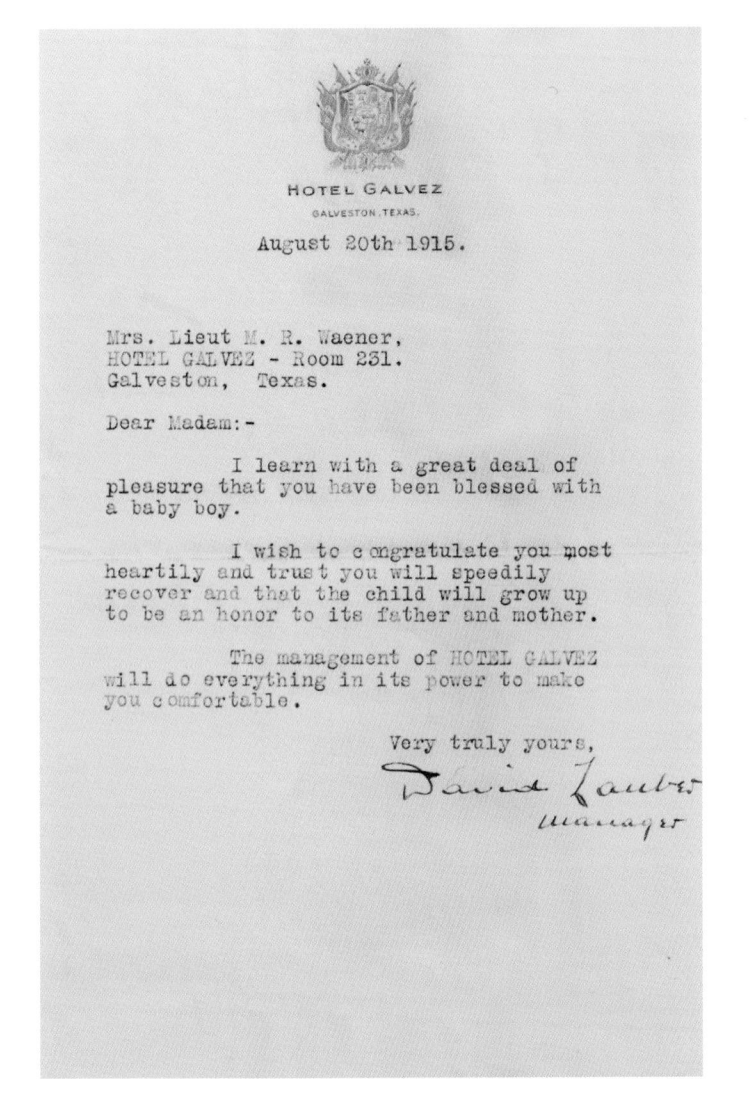

Opposite: A number of Galvez postcards were popular over the years with guests writing home. Above: David Lauber, the Galvez's manager, wrote to congratulate the parents of Max Wainer, who was born in the hotel during the 1915 hurricane.

THANKS FOR THE MEMORIES

The Hotel Galvez and Spa lives eternally in the memories of thousands of people who have been its guests over a century. The following are a few of the mementoes they have shared with us.

1915
Lawrence A. Wainer
Dallas, Texas

My father, Max Wainer Sr., was born in the Hotel Galvez, in Room 231, during the 1915 storm. (Room 231 was located where the elevator bank now stands.) I have a copy of his birth certificate and a letter from the general manager of the Hotel Galvez, written in 1915, congratulating the parents on the new arrival and assuring them that the Hotel Galvez would take care of them.

1926
Dr. E. Sinks McLarty
Galveston, Texas

We moved to the Galvez in 1926, when I was about five. The hotel back then had a lot of permanent residents. Times were hard and a lot of people worked for the hotel and lived there, too. Pop was the hotel doctor. Even though my dad was the doctor, we were too poor to eat at the hotel. We got our meals at a boarding house a few blocks away. You learn to eat fast at a boarding house.

We lived in three rooms in the middle section of the sixth floor, on the south side, overlooking the Gulf. Sam Maceo had his penthouse on the floor just above us. Sam was a good man, really nice to me. He had a nephew about my age who stayed at the Galvez sometimes. His nephew had a secret hiding place inside one of the closets where you could look into people's bedrooms, but I was always afraid to go with him. They said that Sam was a gangster. I don't know about that. Someone had to keep the town clean and orderly, otherwise people wouldn't come here to gamble. The thing is, everyone had a good job and everyone seemed happy.

All the permanent guests had a little space up in the attic to store things. I'd go up there to play or shoot pigeons with my BB gun. I walked over every inch of the roof and knew all the hiding places in the basement. That's where I kept my bike, in the basement. I'd make these balsam-wood airplanes and fly them in the big ballroom when no one was in there. Or I'd go up to the roof and watch them fly airplanes over at Fort Crockett on Forty-fifth Street. A lot of times people who lived at the hotel would be away somewhere and I'd have the whole lobby to myself. I'd take naps on the couches. Everyone in the hotel was my babysitter.

The elevator was open back then, just a metal cage. The stairwell was open, too. Walking down the stairs, you'd see this picture of some important person on the landing; I thought it must be the mayor. There were slot machines, too, lined up by the newsstand where they sold magazines, cigars, and punch boards. I remember the gal who ran the newsstand: she must have had a sugar daddy because she owned a streamlined automobile that could go 101 miles per hour. And you'd see these Third Air Force hotshots in their spats, parading around like they owned the world.

Most of the rooms on the sixth floor didn't have bathrooms. There was this one bathroom down the hall from us, behind the elevator, that nobody ever used. I ordered this alligator from a catalogue and kept him in the bathtub. Well, he got out one day and created quite a ruckus. I could hear my dad shouting, "What's going on down there?" and I'd tell him, "Oh, nothing." I must have been a pain to other people. I know I was a problem because after grade school they sent me off to a military academy in Gainesville, Florida. Best thing that ever happened to me, by the way: they let me know there were rules that had to be followed.

After the Army Air Force [during World War II], I came back to the Galvez to practice with my dad. Our office was on the lower level, just below the Music Hall. We had a general practice, a lot of surgeries, and were open to the public, not just hotel guests. At first there was a separate entrance and a separate waiting room for black people, but we changed that. Color didn't matter. They were all sick, so we put them in the same waiting room and they got along great.

About 1960 we ended our practice at the Galvez and opened our own clinic.

1927
Priscilla Ervin
Arlington, Texas

My grandparents from Fort Worth, Roy Robert Brown and Minnie Warren Pemberton Brown, spent their 1927 honeymoon at the Hotel Galvez. All through my childhood, I heard about how lovely the hotel was. In 1933 they returned to Galveston to live for several years. On their fiftieth wedding anniversary, they returned for a stay at the hotel, a very memorable trip for them, indeed!

1928
Idaleene Scheu Fuqua
Denton, Texas

It was July 1928 when my father, Fred H. Scheu, a Santa Fe station agent in Wayne, Oklahoma, took his family on a vacation to Galveston. Mother ordered our bathing suits from the Montgomery Ward catalogue . . . red for my brother and me so we could be seen on the beach and black for herself and Daddy. All the suits were made of wool, so we could stay warm in the water. I had a red rubber bathing cap with little white bunnies running around it, and mother had a blue one with a white wing on it.

Grandmother Ender, whom we picked up in Waco, had never had a bathing suit in her life; she rented one from a bathhouse at the beach. Grandmother joined a senior group one day and they picked up shells on the beach.

We stayed at the Galvez, the first hotel I ever stayed at, but it would not be the last, as I spent fifty-five years in the commercial air and travel business.

1930
Noel Newton Templer
Dallas, Texas

My aunt and uncle, Mary Jane Newton (my father's sister) and Eugene McDaniel of Hubbard, Texas, were married in Dawson, Texas, home of the bride's parents, on June 30, 1930. The McDaniels spent the first night of their honeymoon at the Galvez and then sailed from there to Cuba. As I remember, Uncle Gene and his family had always stayed at the Galvez in the summers. Numerous friends of theirs would join them each summer for their annual trek to the Galvez and the beach in the 1930s and 1940s.

From the late Forties through the Fifties, we would spend each July at the Galvez for a week with all the women in the family. We never stayed anywhere else. We would get up anywhere from 2:00 to 4:00 A.M., before it got too warm, load everything in the Roadmaster or Fleetwood, and drive the distance on a two-lane highway, through downtown Houston, and would arrive at the Galvez by late afternoon. The bellmen were so nice and always remembered us. We always had a room facing the water.

I remember the large rooms with the ceiling fans and open windows, because there was no air conditioning. I think we went down the hall to the baths. Large attic fans in the halls provided more than adequate

Opposite top: Dr. E. Sinks McLarty was a resident of the hotel from the age of five until he was a teenager and later practiced medicine here with his father. Bottom: Roy Robert Brown and Minnie Pemberton Brown spent their honeymoon in 1927 at the Galvez. Top: Idaleene Scheu Fuqua, pictured with the straw hat on the far right, was four years old when she and her family vacationed here in 1928. For the trip, her mother ordered wool bathing suits from Montgomery Ward for the whole family. Above: A vintage matchbook features a colorful Hotel Galvez on its cover.

GHOSTS AND OTHER GUESTS · 121

ventilation. When all the women went, we got adjoining rooms. When I went with my aunt and uncle, they put a cot in their room for me.

We would always have breakfast at the hotel before going to the beach. We would then walk across the street, sun until about 11:30, and have lunch at the Dream Cafe, watching the gulls swarm.

Sometimes we would drive to Gaido's or John's for lunch or dinner or perhaps just walk back across to the Balinese Room at night. I remember putting on my little white gloves and dressing to the hilt for dinner at the Balinese. It was so exciting. We always had reservations waiting for us at the Balinese, because my uncle knew the Fertittas and the Maceos personally and spent quite a bit of time with them over at the Balinese before they shut down the gambling. He told many interesting stories about that era and all the people and good times.

Each July I still feel the call of Galveston, but I know it would not be the same. Each time I go back to the Galvez lobby, I feel all of my family looking down, smiling and happy, and I fondly reflect on the memories of when we were all able to enjoy such special times.

1944
James R. "Bob" and Virginia M. Humphreys
Fairview, Texas

In 1944, after receiving my wings as an army pilot in Texas, my fiancée and I drove all night back to Tulsa and held our big wedding in the Presbyterian Church on June 30. My orders gave me a nine-day delay en route to my first base at Del Rio, Texas, so we scheduled our honeymoon in Galveston. We arrived at the Hotel Galvez on July 1.

At that time in front of the Hotel Galvez there was a long wharf that extended from the seawall out into the Gulf. Being young newlyweds, we decided the first night to celebrate at the wharf restaurant and maybe even gamble a little. We were dressed up in our summer holiday clothes and knocked on the entrance, ready for a good dinner and entertainment. We were turned away with the words, "You kids cannot come in here!"

With that, we went back to our room, changed clothes into my uniform and a beautiful dress for my wife, and knocked on the entrance door again. The same man said, "Good evening, sir and madam. Please come in and enjoy your stay."

Obviously, the World War II uniform with silver wings and the silver eagle on my hat, plus my beautifully dressed young bride, did the trick—because then we were only twenty-one and nineteen!

1945
Jeanette Leonetti
Houston, Texas

In 1945 my parents, Ralph and Shirley Leonetti, spent their honeymoon at the Hotel Galvez. As they walked to the front desk they tried to pretend they weren't nervous or shy to check into a hotel for about the first time in their lives. The desk clerk requested the name for the reservation and invited my father to sign the register. Dad asked my mother if she would like to do it. This would be the first time she would be writing her new married name. Mom said that, as she was trying to be so poised and calm, she took the pen in her hand and as she bent her head down to sign rice spilled all over the desk counter from her wide-brimmed hat!

Well, so much for being coy!!

Happy 100th birthday, Hotel Galvez.

1948
James F. Anderson
Lancaster, Texas

My memory of the Hotel Galvez in November 1948 is neither romantic nor exciting. As a matter of fact, my stay at the hotel was boring. Here's why:

After serving in World War II, I graduated from Southern Methodist University in Dallas and was hired by the U.S. Treasury Department as an internal revenue agent. The department scheduled a six-week course in income tax regulations at the Hotel Galvez. So I endured six five-day weeks in one of the hotel's conference rooms, studying tax laws.

I shared a room with another agent for one week. Our travel allowance was very meager, so we spent the rest of our time in Galveston at the Seawall Hotel down the beach. I am fortunate, at the age of eighty-five, to still have an active mind and remember the days at the Hotel Galvez.

Opposite top: Galvestonians Sophie and Joe Hurley enjoy the beach near the Balinese Room, which is pictured in the background. Bottom: An old room key is one of the mementoes left from the hotel's early years. Above: James R. Humphreys and his wife, Virginia, enjoyed a 1944 honeymoon at the Hotel Galvez after he received his wings as an army pilot.

1961
Gayle Wilkinson
Midlothian, Texas

When I graduated from high school in 1961, my parents and the parents of three of my friends allowed us to take a graduation trip by ourselves. We each had $50 cash. The mother of one of my friends let us use her second car and provided us with a fuel card that we used to buy gas. We paid her back later with money from our jobs when we returned.

My mother made us reservations at the Hotel Galvez. We could stay until our money ran out. I do not remember what the rate per night for the room was. But there were four of us, and there was one bed. When we arrived we put the amount of money that five days would cost in the hotel safe. We were determined to stay in Galveston for five days. What was left over was our spending money.

We ate one meal a day . . . sometimes breakfast (which was cheap) and the rest of the time at the Jack Tar Hotel cafeteria. One night we ate at Gaido's. When we ate at the Jack Tar, we would have one item . . . usually a baked potato for me, which I think cost ten cents.

We took turns sleeping three on the bed and one on the couch that was in the room.

We spent most of our days on the beach. At night we rode the elevator up and down at the hotel, or just sat in the lobby. There was a postmasters convention going on, so we had the opportunity to chat with the attendees. One night some of the gentlemen invited us to come up to the penthouse. We rode up the elevator, got off at the penthouse, walked around it once, and got right back on the elevator and came back downstairs. We were horrified at how stupid we were to assume that it was okay to go up there where there was nothing but a room full of "old men"!

That was the most daring thing we did on our trip.

I had never stayed in a hotel before, so this was an adventure that for me felt like being Alice in Wonderland there at the grand Hotel Galvez.

After five nights we checked out, using the money we had left in the safe. We had no money to buy food for the trip back to Fort Worth, but we didn't care. It had been a wonderful week, filled with memories that are with me still. It's proof that in 1961, one could spend five days at a vacation resort with just $50.

1961
Leo G. Stanich
Galveston, Texas

My father and mother were BOIs (born on the Island) and members of the Galvez Club many years ago. My father passed away in 1952, so that gives you an idea of how long my family has been associated with the Galvez. I still remember our club membership number: 1594.

I remember when I was a youngster at the pool ordering a hamburger and a Coke and thinking how grown up I felt giving them our club number and signing for it. My sister, Diane, and I practically grew up at the Galvez pool. A young lifeguard named Ed Hinkle taught me to swim there. Diane can't remember the name of the gentleman who taught her to swim, but she remembers the teen room downstairs, which was a gathering place for young people. It had ping-pong tables and a juke box. She had her seventh birthday party at the Galvez.

One of my most vivid memories was staying there during Hurricane Carla in 1961. My mother felt that the hotel was a good, solid, safe place to stay during the storm. When we checked in there were was a gigantic bowl of fresh fruit on a table in the lobby. This was quite an adventure for a nine-year-old, and until the storm hit with full force I roamed the hotel freely.

In the eastern part of the hotel, what was called the Villa [the motel], there was a huge picture window and that's where people gathered to watch the Gulf waters churn and rise. What a sight to watch the huge waves come crashing over the seawall. As conditions worsened, this area was closed and we went back to our rooms; my mother, sister, and grandmother and I had adjoining rooms. During the height of the storm, we heard a loud crash, which we found out later was a tornado hitting the corner of the hotel where our room was. Before, after, and during the storm, everything was done to make sure the guests were as comfortable as possible.

Over the years there have been many more memories: my sister's elegant wedding reception in the Grecian Room in 1969, for example. I know there will be many more.

Opposite top: Gayle Tucker Wilkinson and her friends celebrated their high school graduation at the Hotel Galvez in 1961. Wilkinson sneaked into a Gulf-view room to take this photograph. Center: Diane Turner, Maurine Gale, and Pam Parker pose in front of the hotel. Bottom: The beach beauties include Diane Turner, Maurine Gale, and Gayle Tucker Wilkinson. Above: During Hurricane Carla, which struck Galveston in 1961, hotel guests were made to feel "as comfortable as possible" before, during, and after the storm. Elsewhere on the Island, people were not so lucky.

1961
Jan Johnson
League City, Texas

The wind was already gusting when my grandparents, my parents, and I checked into the Hotel Galvez mid-afternoon the Saturday before Hurricane Carla in 1961. (I was eight years old, but my memories are still vivid.) We got the last two rooms. My parents and I had one with a Gulf view on the third or fourth floor, and they put the two twin beds together for the three of us. Mom immediately started filling the bathtub with fresh water to drink and flush the toilet.

After these preparations, we went down to the lobby, which was filled with refugees who could not get rooms. Some of them were my classmates and had brought their pets, which we had been told were strictly forbidden. Our Siamese cats stayed home, but KHOU's Gene Broadrick had smuggled his in. He hosted a weekly Sunday-morning show on Galveston; its theme music was Dvořák's *New World Symphony*. Another broadcaster from Channel 11, Dan Rather, was also at the Galvez, and Mr. Broadrick introduced him to us in the lobby.

Hotel staff emptied the pool to use for the same purpose as our bathtub water. Because the hotel was more than full, every meal was served military style in the enclosed dining room from a buffet line. Not knowing what awaited us, everyone seemed to adopt a "we're-all-in-this-together" attitude to ride out the storm together. The rest of that Saturday and Sunday passed in a waiting-and-watching mode, mostly in our hotel room in front of the small television. For the first time, a radar screen was broadcast on TV, and we watched as the eye of the storm moved closer and closer to the Island, aiming to make a direct hit.

Sunday night (or maybe Monday night, or both), my parents entertained all their theater buddies in our room with poker and much liquor—my first hurricane party. Unfortunately, I fell asleep early to its background noise. Mom said that it went on until 1:00 or 2:00 A.M. Sometime after that, she awoke and looked out the window to see Ranger's Run at the Balinese Room fall into the Gulf before passing out again. At some point, she also noted the waves crashing over the seawall onto the wide lawn of the Hotel Galvez. On Monday morning, when we went down to breakfast, we heard a terrific crash from the lobby's west side: one of the floor-to-ceiling glass windows in the Grecian (now Music) Room had crashed in. The room was immediately sealed off from all guests.

Back up in the room, we watched TV as Hurricane Carla made a definite jog to the west of Galveston Island. Even as the electricity cut off, a general sigh of relief was heard, but the storm wasn't over yet. That night, while we were sleeping, a waterspout came ashore just two blocks west of us. The tornado literally bounced down Twenty-third Street before veering over to Twenty-first, where it destroyed the original Rosenberg Elementary School, built during the 1880s.

Tuesday dawned still cloudy but much more calm. I was growing bored by now and ready to go home, but we were told that city workers had to check things out before they would give the "all clear." I remember sitting on my father's lap in the second-floor Villa on the east side of the Galvez, overlooking the seawall. The street was covered to its curb with Gulf water and I could see fish and jellyfish swimming beneath its surface. After the electricity and phone service were restored, Dad called our neighbors to see how our rented house fared. With their worst fears uppermost in their minds, my parents waited. An excited voice on the other end reported, "Oh, no! Your TV antenna is down!"

And that was the worst for us. We went home that night.

2001
Kathryn Straach
Dallas, Texas

Where were you September 11?

I was with an old friend I have known since childhood. She gave me shelter as I watched the terrifying and heartbreaking events unfold in New York, Washington, and Pennsylvania.

My friend is the Hotel Galvez in Galveston.

My parents introduced her to me when I was young. I clearly remember toting buckets of sand from the beach across the street and dumping them into the bathtub of our suite. (I was fascinated by the sea creatures that burrow into the sand.) I sure hope my parents tipped the maid well.

I returned with my parents as a teenager and spent a memorable afternoon at the pool, flirting with a boy I ended up corresponding with for quite a while after that trip. At that time, the pool was the more traditional rectangular shape and was in front of the hotel. Now off to the hotel's side, the pool is lagoon shaped, with a swim-up bar—a setting worthy of other teenage romances.

Opposite: Howard Decker worked as an engineer to air condition the Hotel Galvez in the 1950s. A family photograph captures the Decker family enjoying the beach across from the hotel. Left: The Deckers would stay in the Galvez Villa, located on the hotel's east side, during their extended visits. This section of the hotel offered shuffleboard and the pool.

My husband and I stayed at the Galvez with our two sons on our first family vacation. We crossed the same street as a family and splashed in the water at the same spot where I had as a kid. I kept a close eye on the boys to make sure that no sea creatures were relocated to our hotel room.

We betrayed my old friend on our honeymoon, staying down the street at the seemingly more exciting Flagship Hotel that stretches over the water.

For our first anniversary we returned to Galveston and, short on money, spent one night on the beach and the next in a motel. I eyed the Galvez longingly as we drove past.

Although the Galvez was built in 1911, she has worked hard to keep up her stunningly good looks by having the occasional facelift. She is beautiful and easily holds her own against the island's newer San Luis and Moody Gardens Hotels.

And she has a sense of humor, as evidenced on the first part of my most recent visit. I was in the city to attend a meeting at the Galvez. My sister-in-law, Janell, was already in town and decided to extend her trip and stay with me.

When I arrived at the hotel, the desk clerk informed me that I had been upgraded to a suite, where Janell awaited me. The clerk escorted me to room 703. The large plaque outside the door trumpeted Honeymoon Suite.

Janell heard me arrive, threw open the door, and greeted me with a hearty, "Hi, honey!"

The accommodations were romantic, but I was there with the wrong Straach.

She had already ordered a rollaway bed, so the staff knew there was trouble in paradise. The maid was confused about how many mints to leave. (She left three.)

It's just as well we weren't honeymooners. Newlyweds might not have noticed the scaffolding blocking the view of the Gulf, but they probably would not have liked the men working right outside the window. (My friend does like to keep up her appearance.)

On our last morning, as Janell and I packed, the television droned its usual morning lineup. Suddenly, terror came into our sanctuary. We watched in horror as an airplane flew into the World Trade Center.

The pictures of destruction are seared into our memories. It's one of those defining moments: You always remember where you were when you learned of the tragic incident.

Some explanation will be needed when I say that I was in the honeymoon suite of the Hotel Galvez on September 11.

But I was with my dear old friend. History was being made, and our history together was adding a chapter. May there be more, and may they end more happily.

Adapted from Kathryn Straach's "Texas Travels" column, *Dallas Morning News*, October 14, 2001. Reprinted with permission.

Opposite: Colonel Henry Wilcox McGowen brought his bride, Novia, to honeymoon at the Hotel Galvez in 1931, a visit captured in a photograph taken at Murdoch's Pier. *Above:* Henry Wilcox McGowen III followed the lead of his grandfather and enjoyed his honeymoon with his new bride, Suzanne, at the Hotel Galvez in 2002.

2002
Suzanne and Henry Wilcox McGowen III
Brownwood, Texas

On the eve of June 1, 2002, my husband and I waltzed across the lawn at the Hotel Galvez, which has threaded through our family over two centuries. My husband's grandfather and namesake, Colonel Henry Wilcox McGowen, U.S. Army, brought his young bride, Novia, to honeymoon at the hotel in 1931.

The next century found my husband kneeling on the jetty in front of the hotel on Valentine's Day. As the waves crashed and the sun set, he pulled out a crystal slipper he had bought in Ireland. In it was a ring and a promise of love. After many tears of joy and of course a "yes" from me, we enjoyed a private moment in a quiet sunroom of the Hotel Galvez. My husband, who was working in legal development in Kosovo, had planned this day from afar with help from the wonderful concierge, Jackie Hasan. She had a lovely place set up for us and was in on the surprise of my sweetheart's arrival back in the States to whisk me off my feet.

Almost four months later, we had our rehearsal dinner at the Hotel Galvez, were married in Trinity Episcopal Church of Galveston, and had our reception at The Tremont House. After a lovely carriage ride from The Strand to the seawall, we found ourselves waltzing across the lawn of the Hotel Galvez, where we spent the first two nights of our marriage. After eight wonderful years and one sweet child, I still feel like our feet are gliding across time.

2008
Michael and Joyce Ann Daniel (BOI)
Galveston, Texas

George Mitchell of the Hotel Galvez has done much good for Galveston Island and has been an inspiration to our Daniel family. Michael and I received annual invitations to George Mitchell's Mardi Gras balls. Because of Hurricane Ike's damage to The Tremont House, the 2009 Mardi Gras Ball, "An African Adventure," was held at the Hotel Galvez that year. Even though we, too, were greatly affected by this devastating storm, Michael and I were more than ever determined to attend the 2009 Mardi Gras event. It was a most needed fellowship of fun: watching the parade in front, catching beads, having my face painted, listening to the great band, dancing and enjoying the delicious buffets.

Milestones

1785
A survey expedition appointed by Bernardo de Gálvez discovers and names the Bahia de Galvezton after the Spanish colonial governor.

1900
The Great Storm, beginning on September 8, devastates Galveston, which takes years to recover.

1902
Part of the hurricane recovery process includes a long seawall, started this year and completed in 1960 at 10.4 miles long.

1910
The Galveston Hotel Company announces plans for a new year-round beach hotel to take the place of the seasonal Beach Hotel, which had burned in 1898.

Construction of the Hotel Galvez is launched the same year to help restore Galveston's reputation as a tourist destination.

1911
The hotel opens for business on June 10 at 6:00 P.M. and soon becomes the choice location for Island residents' galas and celebrations.

1915
Another hurricane hits Galveston, but the new seawall helps spare the Galvez.

1918
The hotel welcomes 40,000 guests at a daily rate of $2.

1928
The Baker Corporation purchases the Galvez for $1 million and undertakes a modernization program.

1931
Ike Kempner and his partners, the original backers, repurchase the hotel.

1937
President Franklin D. Roosevelt makes the Galvez his official Summer White House while he fishes offshore on his yacht, the U.S.S. *Potomac*.

1940
W. L. Moody Jr. and his National Hotel Corporation purchase the hotel from the Kempner group and undertake new renovations. A swimming pool is added, along with a modern motel on the hotel's east end and the members-only Galvez Club.

1942
The U.S. Coast Guard commandeers the Galvez and uses it as its wartime headquarters for the next two years, including as staff living space.

The Sui Jen nightclub, owned by the racketeer Sam Maceo, is renamed the Balinese Room and becomes the most popular nightclub on the Texas coast.

1957
The Galveston rackets are closed down in an Island-wide raid on gambling casinos.

1961
Hurricane Carla, second in intensity only to the Great Storm of 1900, wreaks damage on the Island.

1971
Moody sells the Galvez for $1 million to its fourth owner, Harvey McCarty, the first owner with no ties to Galveston, who partnered with Leon Bromberg, a BOI.

1976
George Mitchell purchases the Thomas Jefferson League Building and renovates it as the first of many restoration projects in The Strand.

1978
The Galvez is closed for renovations and reopens the next year under a new owner, the Mariner Corporation, and a new name, the Galvez Marriott.

1979
The National Register of Historic Places adds the hotel to its list of significant landmarks.

1983
During Hurricane Alicia some guests take refuge at the Galvez, which reopens the next year after significant damage is repaired.

1985
Mitchell converts the Blum Building in The Strand into a new Tremont House and launches his new hotel with a revival of the Island's historic Mardi Gras festivals. The previous year he had built another hotel, the San Luis, on top of the historic Fort Crockett's bunkers, along the seawall.

1988
The Galvez is sold at auction after its owners declare bankruptcy. Aetna Life Insurance Company, the mortgage holder, takes over for $7.68 million.

1993
Mitchell Historic Properties purchases the hotel from Aetna for $3 million and undertakes a $20 million upgrade that restores the public spaces to recall their 1911 appearance.

1996
Wyndham International is retained to manage and operate the Galvez as part of the Wyndham group of premier historic hotels, called Wyndham Grand Hotels.

2002
The Galvez becomes a member of the Historic Hotels of America, a consortium sponsored by the National Trust for Historic Preservation.

2005
A second renovation of the hotel, directed by the Mitchells' daughter Sheridan Mitchell Lorenz of Austin, removes heavy drapes obscuring the Gulf views and restores the windows on the lobby level to their original appearance. Fabrics and carpets are also updated; the Oleander Garden is launched; and planning is begun for the hotel's first spa.

2008
The Spa at the Hotel Galvez opens in the space originally occupied by the hotel's barbershop and drugstore.

Hurricane Ike comes ashore, damaging many Galveston buildings; the Mitchells step in to help direct repairs, including the quarter of The Strand's buildings that are owned by their company.

2009
Credited with launching the renaissance of Galveston's historic downtown, George Mitchell receives the Spirit of Galveston Award from the Galveston Chamber of Commerce.

2011
The Queen of the Gulf observes it centennial with a year-long celebration. Activities include a Spanish cultural evening celebrating the birthday of Bernardo de Gálvez, a mass wedding vow renewal for former guests who were married at the hotel, outdoor concerts, and fireworks.

Acknowledgments

I am indebted to the many wonderful historians who have researched and written about Galveston and the Hotel Galvez over the years, as well as to the many people who talked with me or wrote letters recalling their family visits to the famous hotel. In particular I would like to thank Dr. E. Sinks McLarty of Galveston, who shared with me his boyhood memories of the hotel and life on the Island, and Nick Kralj, the Austin political consultant who recalled for me his days as lifeguard and pool manager at the Galvez. Thanks, too, to the staff of the Rosenberg Library who assisted in my research and to the archivist of the *Galveston Daily News*.

I'm especially grateful to George Mitchell, whose vision, generosity, and love for Galveston made possible the renovation of this Island treasure, and to his daughter Sheridan Mitchell Lorenz, whose help was invaluable to this book. I would also like to acknowledge the architects Boone Powell and Michael Gaertner, who supervized the hotel's most recent renovation in the 1990s; Christine Hopkins, the public relations manager for Mitchell Historic Properties; Jackie Hasan, senior concierge and historian at the Hotel Galvez; and Larry Wygant, who did much of the initial research for this book.

Gary Cartwright

The Hotel Galvez would like to thank the following Galveston historians and curators for their assistance with research and photographs for this book: Casey Greene, Galveston and Texas History Center; Jodi Wright-Gidley and Jennifer Marines, Galveston County Historical Museum; and Karen Guernsey, Moody Mansion and Museum. We also want to recognize Dr. E. Sinks McLarty for his personal insight, as well as all the individuals who took the time to submit their memories and photographs for consideration for this book and the hotel's Hall of History. Special thanks are also due George Mitchell and the Mitchell family for their commitment to preserving Texas's Queen of the Gulf.

Renee Adame and Christine Hopkins

Illustration Credits

All historic photographs, postcards, and other illustrations are from the Hotel Galvez Collection, and all color photography is by Carol M. Highsmith, except as indicated below:

Richie Adoue: p. 63 bottom second from the left; Joan Allred: pp. 112–13; Robert Bear III: p. 65 top; Bridgeman Art Library: p. 115 bottom left; Calvis Bryant: p. 68 top; Linda Fitzgerald Cain: p. 68 bottom left; Adeline Casey: p. 132; Paul Cisneros, p. 24; Wayne Cox: pp. 111 top; Barbara Craft, Hotel Galvez Collection: p. 104; Love Decker: pp. 126, 127; Casey Dunn, Hotel Galvez Collection: p. 38 top; Helen Eaton: p. 122 top; Priscilla Ervin: p. 120 bottom; Idaleene Scheu Fuqua: p. 121 top; Galveston Convention and Visitors Bureau: p. 53; Galveston County Historical Museum: pp. 18, 19, 63 bottom right, 83 top, 125; Galveston Historical Foundation: pp. 99, 103; James and Virginia Humphreys: p. 123; Islanders by Choice: pp. 84–85 bottom; Library of Congress: pp. 58 bottom (Griffith and Griffith), 59 (B. L. Singley, Keystone), 61 top left, 62–63 top and center, 114 top left (Elias Goldensky), 114 top right, 114 bottom (Thomas J. O'Halloran, *U.S. News & World Report*), 115 center left (U.S. Army), 115 center (United Press International), 115 center right (Office of War Information), 115 bottom center (Harris and Ewing); Suzanne McGowen: pp. 128, 129; Robert Mihovil, Mitchell Historic Properties: pp. 96–97, 103, 104–5, 106–7; Moody Mansion and Museum: p. 68 center top; Jennifer Reynolds, Hotel Galvez Collection: pp. 44 bottom left, 50–51, 51 top, 71, 110; Rosenberg Library, Galveston, Texas: pp. 30 top left, 48–49, 50, 51 top, 55 bottom left and right, 58 top, 60, 63 bottom left and second from right, 64, 66, 69 top right, 78–79, 80–81, 82, 83 bottom, 84 top and center, 85 top left, 86 bottom right, 87, 88, 92, 94, 95, 111, 115 top; Christine Sorenson: p. 38; Terry Vine, Hotel Galvez Collection: jacket and pp. 32–33, 40, 42–43, 47, 100–101; Lawrence A. Wainer: p. 119; Jimmy Webb: p. 115 bottom right; Gayle Wilkinson: p. 124.

Display Pages

Endpapers: A montage of the Spanish coats of arms lining the hotel's loggia.

1: The cover of a Hotel Galvez brochure published to promote its opening.

2–3: The four towers that crown the landmark's central section.

4: The lobby's gold-plated mailbox and a pilaster capital inscribed with G for Galvez.

5: One of a pair of sculpted figures above the Music Room's entrance doors.

6–7: The front of the hotel captured in a postcard after its 1911 opening.

8–9: Tall arched windows in the east loggia. Inset: A postcard showing the loggia a century ago.

10–11: The Music Room on the west side, ready for a party. Inset: A postcard with the same space lavishly decorated for a celebration.

12–13: An aerial postcard of Seawall Boulevard showing the Hotel Galvez behind an entrance landscape of palm trees.

14–15: The restored Hutchings-Sealy Building (1895) in Galveston's historic Strand.

16–17: The lobby and the Lobby Bar seen from the entrance loggia.

20–21: A plan of the hotel's main floor.

22–23: Bikers traveling past the front entrance of the century-old landmark.

48–49: Oil painting *Galveston Wharf Scene* (1885, Julius Stockfleth), the artist's first identifiable Texas work (showing the Twenty-first Street Wharf in the foreground and McKinney's Wharf in the background).

78–79: A 1930 aerial view featuring the hotel's main entrance along Seawall Boulevard.

90–91: Brick detail of a building in Galveston's Strand Historic District.

112–13: A snapshot of the Allred family taken in front of the Hotel Galvez.

132: Anna DePuglio Grady inspecting what appears to be a Curtis JN-4 "Jenny" biplane in front of the hotel.

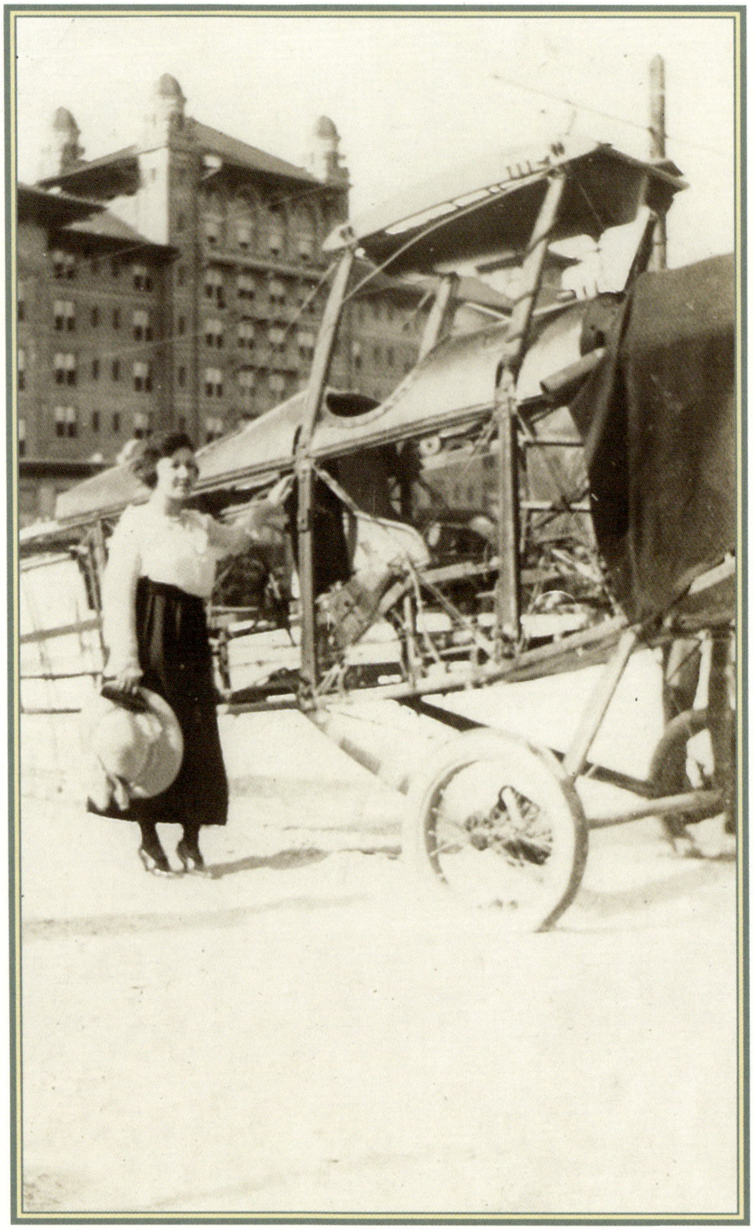

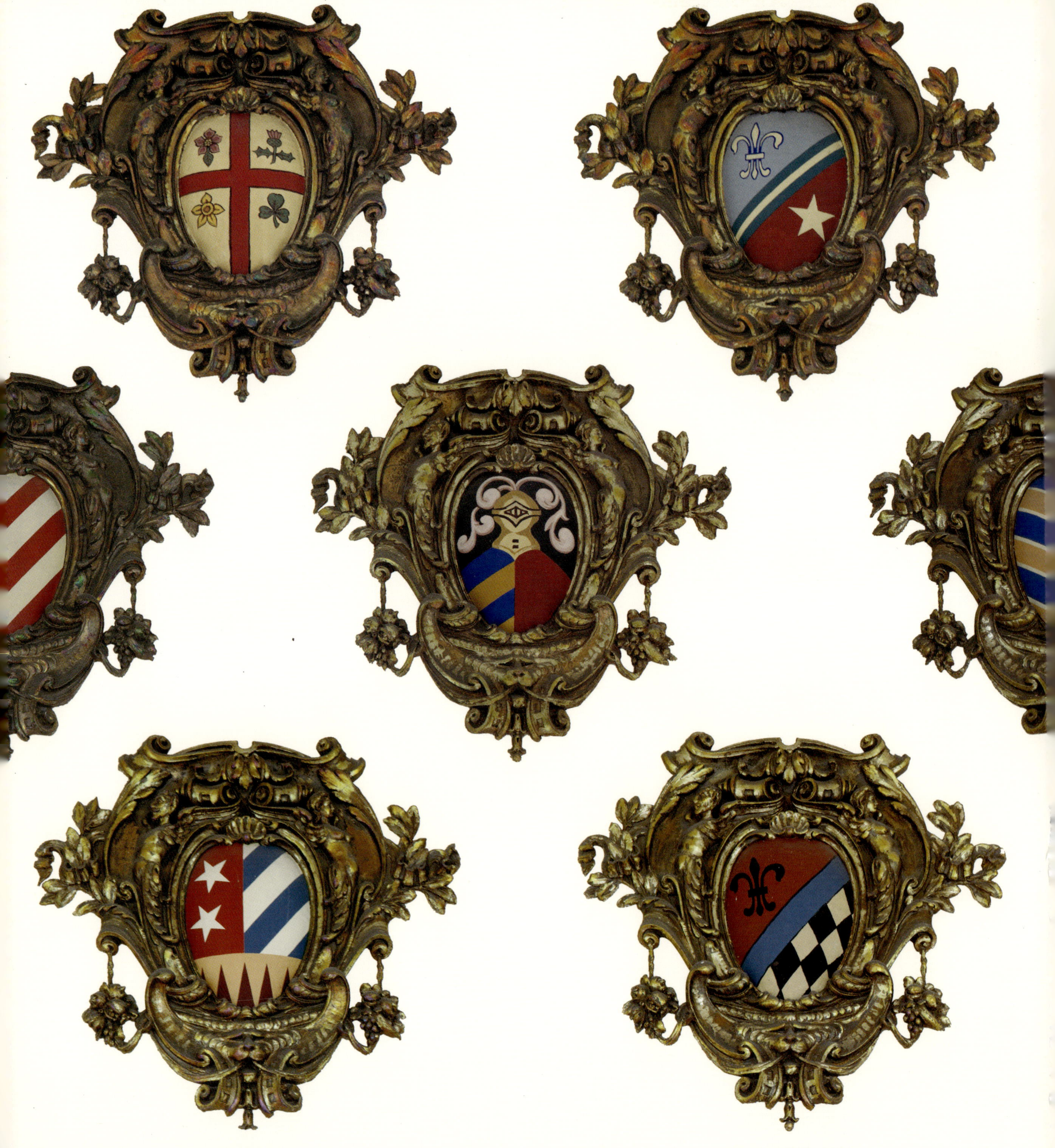